BAY TO OCEAN 2018

The Year's Best Writing from the Eastern Shore Writers Association

EASTON, MARYLAND

Eastern Shore Writers Association
P.O. Box 1773
Easton, MD 21601

www.easternshorewriters.org

Cover art by Lynne Lockhart, used with permission.

CONTENTS

FICTION

NONFICTION

POETRY

PREFACE

Every now and then, the unexpected brings a complete joy.

Sometime last fall, a message arrived I could not have anticipated at all. Would I consider helping select work for a new anthology? I have the good fortune to edit a literary magazine and have edited several anthologies in the past—this is work I love—so it was a message I read happily.

The Eastern Shore Writers Association, I learned, was putting together its first anthology of member work in thirty years. Wonderful, I thought! Yes, I thought. Of course.

I imagine the group at the ESWA selected me because I am a Midwestern prairie kid. I would be an impartial judge. I am quite sure they didn't know I have deep experience and love for the eastern shore. From Boston to Charleston, I have waded in marshes, swam in the ocean, hiked the forests and city streets, and enjoyed every moment. The literature of this region has always had a call to my heart.

My job, of course, was the easy one. Susan Parker, Pat Valdata, Tery Griffin, Emily Rich, and Ron Sauder, members of the ESWA editorial board, read every manuscript before sending their recommendations to me. All the bylines were removed. While the final responsibility for selections was mine, I benefited tremendously from their efforts to promote the project and assemble a fine pool of work from more than two dozen ESWA members. Their work continued after mine, too, to create the physical book you hold in your hands.

The editorial board's insight, taste, love for ESWA and dedication to this project needs to be celebrated.

And what a splendid group of poems and stories and nonfiction they sent. All good literature is transporting—to another time, another place, another way of looking at the world, another articulation of the soul. The best literature is also transformative. It can change the way we view our histories, both shared and private, and it can challenge what we think we know about ourselves. You will find both the transporting and the transformative within this collection

Thank you to the ESWA for allowing me the privilege of this reading. Thank you to every writer who submitted work. To read your work was, and remains, that complete joy. Congratulations to the writers included in this fine act of community and place. And congratulations to everyone who holds this book, open for reading. You're in for a treat.

W. Scott Olsen
Moorhead, Minnesota

FICTION

Jackson Coppley

THREE BOYS AND THE MOVING PICTURES

"Helen, look what I found."

James and his sister Helen were in their grandparent's attic in Sacramento. Their grandparents settled there after Granddad retired from the entertainment business in LA. Both died recently and James and Helen helped their parents go through the old folks' belongings, one of which was the shoebox James now held.

"Look at this," he said as he picked up an old photo lying on top of a notebook in the shoebox.

"Casino? Moving Pictures?" she noted. "Where was this?"

James turned over the photo to show her what was written on the back, "Rehoboth Beach, 1914." "The family in the photo is unidentified, but it's not Granddad's. Must be a publicity photo."

"Rehoboth Beach," Helen scrunched her face in thought. "Isn't that in Delaware where Granddad grew up?"

"I believe so, but look, there's a notebook under the photo. It seems to be something that Granddad wrote."

James began to read from the notebook.

* * *

A friend from childhood passed away recently and I realized memories could be lost forever unless we care enough to share them. So

I'm writing about one day of my life in a small beach town in Delaware that I realize now, as an old man, changed my life.

John, Buster, and I were fast friends. We were neighbors in Sussex County, not the next-door type city boys would be. This was farm country. Your neighbor lived some distance away. So it was with us. We were twelve-years-old. Well, I was the runt at eleven and a half, but we all were in the same class in the little four-room school in that part of the county.

John Nelson, tall and slim, a serious boy, was the oldest of a family of five kids and counting. Mom had three boys and two girls with a baby on the way. Being the oldest, John took the role of his pa's second in command. He was the one who got the cows ready for milking each morning and evening, although his sister Sally, at ten years of age, was coming along fine as the lead milk maid. Theirs was a small dairy farm, with twelve Jersey cows. In those days, before electricity and well before milking machines, relieving the cows of their bounty was by hand and bucket.

Mr. Nelson spent his time raising corn for the cows during growing season and working on the tractor during the winter. Grandpa had a steam tractor he took around to other farms to power threshing machines during harvest and ran a sawmill in the winter. Mr. Nelson grew up helping Grandpa and loved it. He loved working on machines, but the steam tractor, like Grandpa, was retired.

Me, I was the youngest of the gang and John and Buster teased me about my name. Early was an old Dutch name passed down in the family. My Granddad was an Early, as was I. But it was the English meaning that always seemed at odds with my personality. I was the fourth child with three older sisters and me, the first son. Pa joked that his first son wasn't early at all. I was also the one redhead in the family. Ma said Great-Grandma Matilda was a redhead and came from Irish stock. I wondered if she shared the freckles I had across my cheeks.

My family was tobacco farmers. We hired Mr. Nelson to cultivate the fields for us with his tractor, but the rest was work by our own hand. We planted the seeds in the early spring and rigged white burlap over them to protect them as they sprouted into young plants. The whole family would replant the seedlings in the fresh, new-turned soil. Then there was the weeding with more hoeing than I liked. But it was the picking that was the worst. We brought in extra help when the time came for that. The picking came in three to four waves as the leaves matured from the bottom to the top of the plant. I liked what followed the best, when they put up the tobacco in the barns to dry. Pa had two tobacco barns. They looked like log cabins where the builder forgot to dab mud between the logs. That was to allow airflow. I tied the leaves to sticks and handed them up to Pa to place in the top of the barn.

Then the stove was fired up to dry the leaves. We took turns at night sleeping near the barns to keep the fire burning and be sure nothing got scorched. I have fond memories of those balmy fall evenings looking up at the stars and dreaming of the adventures I would have when I grew up.

Buster's family grew cash crops, wheat, barley, some peas when they had a mind to. His pa owned a threshing machine and used John's family tractor to power it. His pa and Mr. Nelson made a business together of taking both machines around to other farms that needed grain separated from the stalk. His pa was a big man, stout and strong, and Buster was too.

If you were around Buster's family, you would hear them call him Henry. 'Buster' is the name John and I gave him when he showed up at church one Sunday wearing a pair of new Buster Brown shoes. He adopted the name for himself since he didn't particularly like the name Henry. But around the family, he remained Henry.

Buster had two brothers eight and ten years older than him and one sister, Dorothy, two years younger. Dorothy was born with something wrong with her legs. She crawled until she was over two years old and then, with her ma working patiently with her, Dorothy stood and walked slowly, but had to hold on to something. She eventually moved around using crutches. Most farm work was beyond her, but she insisted on feeding the chickens and gathering their eggs. In the henhouse, she had things she could hold onto to steady herself. Her pa put in extra handholds just for her.

In spite of her limitations, Dorothy had a smile for everyone. She was a great cook and often presented a fresh apple pie to Buster and his brothers, but Buster knew she meant it for him. He was her protector, or at least he felt that way.

It was a Sunday after church that we learned of our new adventure. Our trio picked at each other, until Mr. Webster became our Sunday school teacher. Mr. Webster was a stern, skinny old man, who didn't tolerate 'monkeyshines.'

Between Sunday school and church, folks gathered on the lawn outside the small white clapboard chapel where buggies and wagons were parked. The only automobile in the neighborhood was the Ford Model T owned by Doctor Price. It was parked outside under an elm tree where I was seated on the grass. I had a piece of plank on my lap and was drawing on the back of a calendar with a pencil. I liked to draw and most folks knew it. They would give me scraps of paper and calendar pages after the month had passed. In return, I drew caricatures of them, which elicited a grin from the recipient, especially if they were a man. I learned to steer clear of drawing women, since they seemed most times to have a notion of themselves that my drawing might offend.

"What're you drawing now?" asked Buster as he walked over to sit beside me. "It's the doctor's Ford," he surmised.

"Yeah," I responded. "Whatcha think?"

"It's good. Hey, why haven't you done one of me?"

"'Cause I don't want to get punched."

"Whatcha mean?" Buster squinted at me.

"'Cause it'll look like your ugly puss."

Buster threw me a punch anyhow.

As we tussled, John came over with news.

"Hey, you two. Stop," he said, with little effect on the wrangling. "Stop," he insisted, "I got news."

"What?" responded Buster, with my head jutting out from the arm grip he held on my neck.

"Want to go to the beach?" he asked, to which Buster released me so we could both pay attention to what John had to say.

Now, you must remember that people didn't journey far in those days. I had gone with Pa to Salisbury to the tobacco auction once and that was an all day journey by horse and wagon. Buster went with his pa and sister to Georgetown once or twice to see what the doctors could do for Dorothy. That was it. The beach was further away and we never had any reason to make the journey. We had never seen the ocean. We were all ears.

"Pa just told me he sold a whole bunch of hay we didn't need," John started as Buster interrupted with, "Yeah, and so?"

"Well, guess who he sold it to?"

"Who?" This time Buster and I responded in unison.

"The ice house in Rehoboth Beach. And he said I could go."

"Lucky you," smirked Buster.

"Hey, I didn't forget my chums," retorted John. "I asked, and he said both of you can go too, if your ma and pa don't mind."

"When?" I asked.

"School's out next week," John said. "We leave right after that."

We wasted no time. Buster and I ran over to our pa's and were doing a lot of excited sleeve pulling and supplication. Each pa grinned at the other. Of course, Mr. Nelson had clued in the other men. They knew they could expect their sons to come running. Mr. Nelson told them he would pay them once in Rehoboth if they did a good job loading and unloading the hay bales. To which Buster's pa responded, "My pa always said if you want a job done in a day, get one boy, if you want it to take longer, get two boys!" Mr. Nelson said he would be sure they behaved.

Buster and I weren't ace students in our class at school. John always beat us on grades. But for the next week, none of us heard what the teacher said. We daydreamed about our time at the beach. Each of us had a different notion of what it was like. John thought the sand would be like that along the creek where we skinny-dip in the summer. He wasn't far from wrong since we did have coastal sand deposits. But the waves we saw in pictures were nothing we could imagine.

After the longest week we ever experienced, school was finally out, and the day came to load the wagon for Mr. Nelson and set off on our adventure. We were used to getting up early to do chores before school, so we had no trouble getting up before dawn. We wasted no time getting to John's house. My ma packed ham biscuits to eat along the way. She added slices of her famous pound cake, the type with a sugar crust on top. I knew I would have to share that treat.

We brought our food in brown paper bags inside flour sacks our ma's had cleaned and scrubbed, along with a fresh set of underwear that we were unlikely to use. Mr. Nelson had already pulled the wagon up to the large barn covered with faded red boards. John was up in the open door of the loft where he set a pulley and rope in place with a large iron piece on the end that looked like an oversized fishing hook.

"Come on boys," Mr. Nelson said to Buster and me as we ran up. "Let's get this wagon loaded and we can set out."

"Yes, sir," we said in unison as we both climbed up in the wagon as John hooked a bale by the twine binding it and swung it out of the loft. Buster and I grabbed the bale as John lowered it and Mr. Nelson squared it up on the wagon. It was hard work, but to us, it was fun and in an hour or two, we had twenty bales on the wagon and Mr. Nelson said it was enough. He brought out two draft horses and harnessed them side-by-side, ready to pull the wagon. He offered John to ride shotgun with him, but John wanted to join his chums in the rear of the wagon behind the bales.

By the time we arrived, the sun was low in the late-spring sky. We arrived at a large brick building with a holding area for last winter's ice flow that had been cut and stored, apparently without sufficient straw for insulation for the summer. Mr. Nelson got out and talked to a man who ran the icehouse. The man smiled at us. He could see how excited we were and said something to Mr. Nelson we didn't hear. Mr. Nelson walked over to us and said, "That man over there is Mr. Henderson. He told me that he had boys who would unload the wagon, so I guess your work is done. Why don't I pay you your wages for the day and let you see the town?"

We were jumping out of our skins with excitement as Mr. Nelson handed a quarter to each of us, our compensation for the day.

"Which way's the ocean?" asked Buster.

"That way," Mr. Nelson said as he pointed down the railroad tracks that ran in the middle of the street. We started to move in that direction but stopped when Mr. Nelson instructed, "Hey, you boys be back here before dark. Mr. Henderson is letting us sleep in his loft. You be careful, hear?"

"Yes, sir," we said together, and we were gone.

Soon, we heard a low, undulating roar new to us. Did the ocean make noise? At the end of the street was the boardwalk. Buster had seen board sidewalks in Georgetown, but this was a wider walk and stretched as far as he could see to the left and right. Just over the boardwalk, there it was, more water than we could imagine, stretching far as the eye could see, and it was not still. No pond we ever saw was in motion like this.

The sand, we expected, but not so much, hills of sand all around.

"Race ya to the water," challenged Buster, and we lit out, but the going was difficult. We were not used to the slipping and tugging of the sand that resisted our progress. We reached the still-wet surface left by the ebb tide, which was easier to navigate. Buster stopped at the water's edge like a bull at a gate, uncertain whether to go forward or not. John and I were less hesitant and I rolled up the legs of my overalls to the knees. John and Buster did likewise and soon enjoyed running through the water that pushed and pulled at you.

Buster stepped out of the waves, looked down and picked up a seashell. He had seen pictures of them in a book his ma had. He remembered how his sister Dorothy would take that book of Ma's down and spend hours looking at the shells. Buster kept a couple of empty snuff bags in his pocket. Never could tell when he would need one for a valuable picked up along the way. He put the shell in the bag and looked for others.

"Whatcha doing?" asked John.

"I'm getting shells for Dorothy."

John and I knew how Buster cared for his little sister and we soon joined in the hunt, picking up specimens for Buster's approval. After much sorting and discarding of inferior objects for the ones considered superior, Buster had a bag full.

The sun was setting, and we realized, with regret, we must head back to the icehouse. As we trudged up to the boardwalk, there stood Mr.

Nelson holding a white paper tote. He was smiling, so we figured we weren't in trouble. Mr. Nelson told us as we set foot on the boardwalk, "I got me something here I thought you might help me with."

John looked into the open bag his pa held out. "What is it, Pa?" he said.

"Salt water taffy. Try a piece."

John looked in the bag and saw lumps of different colors. He took a blue one and popped it in his mouth. Buster and I chose one each. We looked at each other with the mutual expression of 'what is this?' It was sweet like candy, but much stickier.

I proclaimed, "Candy chewing tobacco."

Mr. Nelson laughed. "Well, I guess that's one way of looking at it, but don't spit. Chew it up and swallow."

We had no problem doing so with that piece and the next piece to come before Mr. Nelson put the tote away for later.

As we enjoyed our taffy, we walked with Mr. Nelson down the boardwalk as gaslights began to illuminate the evening. None of us had electricity at home, nor gas, just kerosene lamps so the illumination of the boardwalk was a true wonder in and of itself.

Wonders of the boardwalk left us wide-eyed as we strolled. There were game arcades, clothing stores and food venders everywhere. There was a game where you could throw a baseball at milk jugs and knock them over. We wanted to try, but it cost a penny a toss and we weren't sure we wanted to part with our newly earned money. We headed back up the street to return to the icehouse and passed a building with a big arch with a sign that read 'Casino.'

"Look there!" said John.

"Where?" we asked.

"Where it says 'Casino,'" responded John, although he pronounced it more like the 'Casano' in 'Casanova' rather than the way it was supposed to be. John was a well-read boy, but books didn't tell you how words were pronounced and there weren't even radios in those days. We seldom heard a fancy word said out loud, except from the preacher on Sunday and casino was not in that man's vocabulary.

"What about it?" asked Buster.

"Look what it says: 'Moving Pictures'!"

We were excited. We heard about moving pictures, but never had the opportunity to see one until now. Mr. Nelson headed to the ticket booth and asked about the show. He came back to us.

"The man who runs the place says they have a movie about a dinosaur," he reported.

A dinosaur! Moving! We were ecstatic. We agreed we had to see this!

"But the man says a ticket will cost each of you a nickel," Mr. Nelson warned.

We each had a quarter from our earnings for the day, but, unlike the baseballs at a penny a toss, none of us had any hesitation regarding this investment. We were all in.

Each of us in turn walked up and exchanged our precious quarter for a ticket and two dimes in change. Mr. Nelson ponied up a nickel for himself as well. We thought Mr. Nelson, being grown up and all, must have seen a moving picture before, but we weren't sure. Being a grown up, he didn't show excitement like a boy does.

We were the only ones in the room for the show. It was a small, bare windowless parlor save for ten cane-back chairs and a white sheet stretched tight in the front of the room. A boy that might have been the son of the owner, a few years older than we were, went behind a wall with a square hole cut in it. Soon a bright light shone through the hole in the wall and onto the sheet as the other lights in the room switched off.

Then words on the screen announced the name 'Gertie.' Other words came on that told us a man named Winsor McCay and his friends were traveling to New York City to see a museum. But what happened next astounded us. The next picture was of a gargantuan building that looked like a castle, but rather than a still picture from a book, the camera panned across the length of the building just like you were there and were turning your head. Then, up comes a large open automobile with a gang of men dressed in the fanciest black duds we had even seen. More words came onto the sheet explaining the men's automobile had a busted tire and they planned to spend time inside the museum while the driver fixed it.

Inside the museum, the picture showed the bones of a huge dinosaur. We felt like we were there and I even reached out my hand to touch the bones, but the other boys snickered at me and I put my hand down, embarrassed by my impulse.

Then more words told that this McCay man could draw pictures. That captured my attention for sure. The text reported that McCay bragged he could bring a dinosaur to life and he showed them some paper he flipped in his hands to demonstrate. Then there was what we would call today a cartoon, except this was the first one ever. We didn't know that at the time, but we were absorbed. There was a pen and ink drawing of a brontosaurus introduced as Gertie. She moved as though she was real! More words came up that told us Gertie liked to dance, and then she danced, right there on the sheet in front of us.

There were other antics Gertie did, like tossing another beast into a lake beside them. The beast swam back up and spit a long stream of water at Gertie. It was a riot and we laughed like crazy. Even Mr. Nelson snickered a lot.

There was little sleep at the icehouse that night. We kept talking about Gertie, repeating the story back and forth like none of us had seen it.

Years passed, but we never forgot that night.

John ran the family farm when he grew up, but he bought a cottage in Rehoboth Beach and got there as much as he could during the summer once there were hard surface roads and they owned a fine Buick to make the trip.

Buster continued to be the big brother for Dorothy, even after she married a man from Georgetown and they started a chicken farm. Buster was a partner in the business. Buster passed away years before Dorothy, who lived into her eighties. She died not long before I started writing this memoir. Dorothy's granddaughter reported that when she passed away, there was just one thing on her bed stand besides an assortment of medicine bottles, and that was a small sack of seashells.

In my case, the day at the casino changed my life. I saved my money and, when I was in my early twenties, I headed to California. I learned of a man from Illinois, not much older than myself, who moved to Los Angeles with his brother and they were looking for good artists. Something to do with a character fashioned after a mouse.

* * *

"Wow," said Helen as James finished.

"Yes, wow," repeated James as he looked at the photo. "Were it not for this Moving Picture house, Granddad wouldn't have moved here and none of us would be here. I know that Granddad's last work was on *Fantasia*. Do you think he remembered that Gertie cartoon in Rehoboth Beach when he did that film?"

"I think you have the answer in your hand," said Helen.

Walter F. Curran

FATED COURSE

An eight-year-old girl, large for her age, adorned with curly, brown-blond hair and amazing blue eyes asked me, "Granpa, is that a real museum?"

If not for that question the link to my grandfather would have been forever lost. It has taken one hundred and eighteen years, five generations, to make the connection.

The Rehoboth Beach Historical Society building was on the far side of the parking lot of the playground I had taken her to.

"Yes, it is. Want to see it?"

"It's small." Her only prior experience being the Smithsonian with her parents.

"Museums are like people. They come in all sizes and shapes and if you pay close attention, they're all interesting."

Jumping up, she grabbed my hand. "Let's go."

"Granpa," pointing at a photo of a Tern Schooner beached, port side to the shore, and stranded in Rehoboth circa October 1899, the name on the stern obscured by a breaking wave slamming the starboard quarter, my granddaughter asked, "What's the name of the boat?"

Peering closer, "Falmouth something or other," I replied.Noticeable on the port quarter is a solitary figure, gazing ashore. Until today it and he were a mystery, stuck in time.

When we left the museum, we walked back to the park, hand in hand, youngster leading old man, and sat on a bench. "Did you like the museum?" I asked.

"Yes," breathing excitement. "I could get close to everything. Some of those people's photos look like the one you have on your office desk."

"They sure did. Which one did you like best?"

Jumping up, she stood in front of me. "I liked them all but the boat on the beach made me sad." Pausing, she peered at me and said, "You looked at it a long time. How did it get there?"

Leaning close, I patted her hair gently, "I'll tell you what. Let's go home and look at the photo on my desk and I'll tell you a story about it."

The photo on my desk is that of a tall, stern looking seafarer next to a large woman, dark-skinned, bearing an impish smile. It sits atop a logbook, used as a personal diary. Handing her the photo, I picked up the logbook. "My father, William Warren Coakley, II, gave me these. My grandfather wrote the logbook. It's an amazing story," and I began to read.

They used to call me "Lucky Bill." Not anymore. I am the captain of the Falmouth Maiden. At least I used to be when it was afloat. She's no longer a maiden, either, after the savage manner in which the storm ravaged her. Now she and I are both stuck on this damned beach called Rehoboth and I'm reduced to sentry duty trying to protect the owner's ship and cargo.

Born William Warren Coakley in the year 1866, the last of seven children of Lauren and James Coakley of East Boston, I am the only surviving member of the family. Destined for the sea from the day of my birth, my first job at age eight was a cabin boy on a dilapidated harbor tug. From there, over the course of the next seven years, I worked on various coastal freighters as a deckhand and bosun, studying navigation and reading every book I could with the help of a couple of mates and captains I sailed under. At the ripe age of sixteen, when on a trip in the Caribbean, the mate, Abraham Carney, took sick and died. After the burial, we couldn't carry a body for another two weeks. The captain, a stern but fair man, called me to his cabin.

"Coakley, you're young but capable and seem to be made of stern stuff. If you can pass my navigation exam, I'll let you replace Mr. Carney as Mate, at least for the remainder of this voyage. What say you?"

Dumbfounded at the offer I replied, "I'll do my damndest, Captain!"

For hours, the captain posed questions, and I responded. I surprised him at the depth of my knowledge on the ocean currents. As the evening ended, he called the crew together and informed them I had passed his queries, I was now Mate and they will obey my orders and treat me with the respect warranted.

I stayed with that captain for four years then transferred to another coaster owned by the same company. At the age of twenty-four, I got my first chance as captain and now, at age thirty-three, forlorn, I stare at the stretch of beach, pondering my fate. I wondered if I would ever again command a ship.

A Tern schooner, a hardy three-master of four hundred tons, rigged fore and aft, The Falmouth Maiden was well equipped for the coastal and Caribbean trades as we made our way to New York with a cargo of lumber.

We rode the Florida current north with winds from the west-northwest until Cape Hatteras and went offshore to stay in the Gulf Stream. Due east of Norfolk, Virginia with the wind easing and shifting toward the northeast we went on the starboard tack and sailed northwest by north which, if the weather held, would take us close to the mouth of the Chesapeake Bay. At that point, depending on the wind, we'd have to tack again and push east-northeast paralleling the shore to the mouth of the Delaware Bay. With luck we could keep that course all along the New Jersey shore and thence into New York.

Leaning on the taffrail, savoring the salt air laced with the smell of fresh-hewn lumber in the cargo hold, I reflected on how hard work and luck had taken me so far from my beginnings.

Within hours of tacking to the northwest, the clouds thickened. Rain and higher winds soon followed. By the end of the afternoon watch, seas were rising.

With seas at twenty feet and gusts estimated at forty knots, a full gale, I ordered all hands, seven crew members and a cook to reef the topsails and take in the flying jib. Even with reduced sail, the gusts were heeling the ship hard over. Four bells into the first watch, I called the crew out again, took in all topsails, the forward staysail and after staysail.

The barometer dropped. Near sundown it read 29.2 inches, and judging by the state of the seas, dense foam streaking from the crests, I estimated the wind steady at forty-five knots with gusts much higher, but the old girl had been through similar storms and weathered them well.

I have sailed through such weather many times, yet, now I was nervous, a strange feeling, tightening my shoulders and clawing at my gut. What was different? A foreboding? Weather is unpredictable and fickle so a prudent captain is always tense in severe weather, yet...?

When the wind rotated from north east to east by north, I realized the Falmouth Maiden was riding the front edge of a hurricane. A mariner's nightmare, strong onshore winds close to land.

Navigating by dead reckoning since taking the noon sun-line, the constant change in wind direction made it difficult to gauge leeward drift toward land in such heavy weather. Confident in the past, perhaps overly so, this apprehension was foreign, a nagging wind tugging at my mind, distracting and unsettling.

For now I held fast steering north by east as the wind grew stronger, the sky darker and the seas angrier. Not a church-going man, I said a prayer for the safety of all aboard.

Over the next six hours, the wind shifted more to the north. The eye of the storm was moving out to sea and passing us. Already behind in our delivery date in New York, knowing the owners' oft-repeated mantra of "Time is money, your time our money," I opted to keep on but reduced sail further by lowering the mainsail, reefing the foresail and mizzen sail, striking the regular jib and hoisting a storm jib in its place. We needed these three sails to keep the ship balanced and maintain steerage way. We were running nearly 'barebones'. Even so, the wind was strong enough that the masts and rigging acted as sails and we made slow progress.

I planned to stand still in the middle of the ocean and let the storm pass on by. A fleeting thought: if you want to make God laugh, tell him your plans. Was God listening? Did he hear my earlier prayer? Was he laughing or benevolent tonight?

At the last change of sail, I had taken over the helm. The cook, a woman named Syriana, dark skinned, curly hair, of unknown pedigree and Amazonian size, large but of perfect proportions, approached me and offered, in her lilting accent to go aloft and assist. With all seven men of the crew trimming sails, I was tempted to agree having seen her in the rigging from time to time and witnessed her agility. Instead, I let her take the helm and I went forward to assist lowering the mainsail. When I returned, I shouted, "Thank you for taking the helm," something I never would say to a man.

Touching her forelock, she yelled back, normal conversation impossible in the screech of the gale, "For you, Captain, I'd do anything," catching me by surprise. Such a sign of loyalty touched me, but the personal implication was both evocative and troublesome.

"Granpa?" my granddaughter interrupted my soliloquy.

Peering over my glasses, I replied, "Yes."

"What's evocative mean?"

"It means that the captain found Syriana attractive."

"Oh. Why was he troubles?"

"Good question. He was the captain and couldn't get involved with a crew member."

"Was she his girlfriend?"

Chuckling, "No, not yet. Let me finish the story," and I resumed reading.

Syriana went below and I continued to wrestle with the helm, my thoughts now diverted. Syriana, near as tall as me, was strong, beautiful in a wild, winsome way and possessed a figure any woman would envy, but her best feature was a delightful, impish smile. She was intelligent—a collection of her books hung in a net bag in the galley— and of a caring nature, treating minor ailments of the crew with tenderness.

Early in the voyage I had noticed two of the crew members playing "grab and poke" as she walked by, a game better suited for a tap room. I intended to call them aside, but before I could, Syriana turned, hand on hips and glared at them. Not a word, just stared. They retreated, apologizing. Later I rebuked them, warning them she was a crew member first and foremost and they disrespected her at their peril. I am sure they felt I exerted a proprietary note, but they were wrong. While I admired her womanly attributes, the captain is the captain and can be nothing else when at sea.

Peering again over my glasses, I watched my granddaughter's blue eyes go wide, and she nodded. I think she now understood "troublesome." Adjusting my glasses, I continued.

With the seas now cresting at thirty feet and washing over the foredeck, I ordered the crew into the safety of the after main cabin where I could call down through the voice pipe if I needed them. As captain, I felt it was my responsibility to steer the ship in these extreme conditions but ordered a standby helmsman with me. No one should ever be on deck alone in heavy weather. We both tied off at the waist to a safety line rigged the breadth of the ship between the taffrails.

Syriana came up with the seaman on the first shift and brought me a tankard of hot tea. As she handed me the tankard, her hand lingered on mine, long enough for me to look into her eyes and see her smile. It was a warm beacon in this dank, dangerous night.

As the night wore on, I tried to beat upwind as best I could, knowing we were losing ground to the west, towards landfall.

Bone tired, shoulders aching from grappling with the wheel, I got a spot of relief when Syriana came up again three hours into the watch bringing me victuals. Ordering the seaman to take the helm and her to stand by, I sat on the deck, pelting rain and sea spray tattooing my back as I braced myself against the leeward side of the binnacle. Syriana moved to the windward side of the binnacle, opened her slicker, leaned over and enveloped the binnacle, offering some protection from the rain as I ate the biscuits and salt cod and reveled in the smell of her.

Washing them down with another tankard of tea, I rose, handed the tankard to Syriana, then leaning against the binnacle, relieved myself downwind, both she and the salt spray indifferent and resumed my position at the helm.

I peeked at my granddaughter, wondering if she would comment on him relieving himself, but she either didn't understand or didn't care. No reaction, so I read on.

Dawn. Gray light revealed walls of spume-topped water assailing the ship. The gale, relentless, drove spray like nails into exposed flesh, hands raw and cold, face numb, eyes stung by salt. The ship shuddered and groaned from the relentless pounding of the thirty-foot seas.

I ordered the bosun to go forward and check the hatch covers to make sure they were tight. He was a man with a wife and seven children, and I worried for his safety, but the ship comes first. I watched as he grappled his way forward and breathed a sigh of relief when he returned in half an hour saying all was secure and watertight.

Unsure, a rare feeling, I held steady for a few more hours, hoping the storm would move faster than us and the winds abate as we approached the Delaware Bay.

Near sunset, with the Delaware shore somewhere ahead, I called all hands on deck and prepared to tack. I let off a bit to allow the ship to pick up speed then threw the helm hard to starboard. The bow struggled to come around but stalled when direct into the wind. We slid back, and I turned the helm hard to port hoping the rudder would provide guidance and help push the bow to starboard but it wasn't to be. Twice more we tried to tack and failed. Calling the crew back to the helm, I told them I would jibe the ship around, cautioning them how dangerous this maneuver could be, stressing that the timing must be perfect.

With Syriana beside me at the helm I bore off to port, now on a close reach, the ship picking up speed. As I continued the turn downwind, I saw, too late, there were two problems. First, the foresail boom was rising. The downhaul had broken. Second, the crew had slacked off the sheets on the mizzen too much. As the foresail boom came around, the strain was too much and it snapped. Then the sheet itself snapped. Within minutes there was nothing but rags where the foresail used to be and the remains of the boom, splinters washing about in the scuppers.

Now, with only the mizzen to work with, dragging the stern to port, forcing us to stay on a starboard tack, I worried. As I pondered the situation, the panicked shouting of the crew came through.

"I see breakers ahead, Captain!"

With that I knew the fight was lost. We had run too far west.

The line of breakers, just visible through the rain, stretched from the south to as far north as I could see. I told the crew I planned on laying the ship on the beach with the anchor forward and a kedge anchor aft, dropped to seaward in the hope we could pull ourselves off when the storm abated. The fear in their eyes mirrored my own thoughts but I dare not show it lest they become panicked, a deadly fault when circumstances require quick action.

Sending the bosun and one man forward to the main anchor, I sent four other seamen to rig the kedge anchor. Stationing the last crewman at the storm jib with orders to release the sheet and let go the halyard the instant we let go the anchor, I instructed Syriana to stand by at the mizzen and do the same for that sail. As she walked away, she turned, smiled, nodded her head and continued on. My resolve hardened. Now I was saving Syriana and the ship.

My intent was to land the ship as upright as possible so the keel would take the main impact.

"Let go the anchors," I shouted, dropping my arm. Watching the breakers crash I shouted, "Take a strain," dropping my arm again. They acted in unison, tightening the lines on the bitts. As the anchors chewed into the seabed, I felt a slight drag, enough to pull the ship erect from her port list then she grounded. Thank God! It was sand.

The men from the Rehoboth Life Saving Station arrived and stood above the breaker line. Using a Lyle gun, a small cannon that shot a projectile with a light line attached, they aimed, shot and dropped the line dead on target. The bosun retrieved it then tied off a heavier line the lifesaving crew hauled ashore. We rigged a block and tackle and attached their breeches-buoy with two pulling lines. Ordering the entire crew ashore, I stayed aboard. To a man, they all fled with no argument except Syriana. As the last one to go, she grabbed my head and kissed me, then climbed into the bosun chair, smiled and waved as the life station crew hauled her ashore. I stood, surprised at her effrontery yet pleased at the same time. All night, as the storm abated, I thought of that kiss, that devotion, that fortitude and vowed to not lose faith, despite the dour circumstances.

Once again, little blue eyes interjected, "She kissed him?" eyes wide, hand to her mouth, then giggled. I giggled too. "May I continue?" I asked and blue eyes nodded.

Heeled to port, beached but not broken, if the seams don't split and if we can get tugboats, we may be able to drag her off the beach. Many "ifs" and small consolation, but enough for now.

In the morning light, with wind lessened and seas calming, instead of being in New York unloading our cargo, I stand sentry. There will be no one claiming salvage of the Falmouth Maiden. Ravaged she may be, but she's still my maiden to protect and protect her I will.

Later than day, Syriana and the bosun returned to the ship. After letting them aboard, I went ashore to find a telegraph and contact the owners. I instructed them to pull up the Jacob's ladder and not let anyone else aboard.

After contacting the owners, returning to the ship at sundown, a goodly number of folks were milling about on the beach and asking questions, curious but polite and friendly.

Syriana fired up the galley stove. It was good to see Charley Noble, every sailor's name for the galley smoke stack, belching smoke, a sign of life. After a meager meal of salted beef, biscuits and hot tea, the bosun went to his bunk, and I retired to mine. A gentle rap on the door frame alerted me to Syriana's presence.

"It's warmer here than in the crew's quarters, can I sleep on the deck?"

Knowing the answer should have been no, I acceded. Tentative at first, she told me about her background and how she came to be on board ships. From French Guyana, she ran away with her older brother from a drunken father, her mother having died when she was a year old, and worked their way on a small ship to the Dutch Antilles. The captain, a Dutchman based in Barbados, took pity on her and protected her from his roughneck crew. When they docked, he arranged for Syriana to stay with his wife and help her with their tavern. Being childless, the wife welcomed Syriana, and she soon loved this stranger showing her, for the first time in her memory, kindness and affection.

When Syriana was twenty, her adopted father was lost at sea with all hands, including her brother. Six months later, the mother died from an unknown disease. The local governor confiscated the tavern for unpaid taxes and Syriana worked her way as cook on a ship bound for America. She had been sailing ever since.

Fascinated, both by her and her tale, I listened and talked but lack of sleep over the last forty-eight hours caught up with me. I dowsed the oil lantern, she in her blanket and me in my bunk. The silence loomed like a cloud, yet comforting, knowing she was there only three steps away. As I drifted off, I heard, "My name is pronounced 'Shiriana, Sh.'"

She awoke me with a tap on the shoulder. Pointing to the table, more tea and biscuits.

"Thank you Syriana," emphasizing the "sh" and evoking that

wonderful smile.

Reaching out for her hand I asked, "Why did you kiss me when you left the ship?"

"I wanted to," defiant. "Why didn't you stop me?"

Pausing, "I didn't want to," and we both smiled.

The tugboats took two days to arrive. Two days in which we cleaned up the ship and replaced broken gear. Syriana and I enjoyed long, intimate nights.

Consulting with the tugboat captains, we agreed we would attempt to drag the ship off the beach in the afternoon of the spring tide, in two days' time.

At 1515 hours, the height of the spring tide, with no wind and calm seas, both tugs each took mighty strains on two of the four mooring cables and with a sloshing groan, the ship came free of the sand. Three days later, with four new crew members aboard, we hoisted sail, heaved anchor and sailed for New York, the end of this voyage but the start of a new life voyage with Syriana.

I looked up, took off my glasses and said, "What do you think?"

Smiling that impish smile, blue eyes said, "Granpa, that was a wonderful story. Can we go for an ice cream cone now?"

Kissing the top of her head, "Yes Syriana, a great idea."

David Healey

LAST STAND AT TURKEY POINT LIGHT

The day the Coast Guard troops drove into Turkey Point, Annie Poole stood out in the keeper's yard to greet them, looking much like the lighthouse she stood beside. She was tall and proud, but a little thick on the bottom, as one might expect from a fifty-something widow.

Dubiously, she eyed the two trucks carrying Coast Guard troops as they rolled into the yard beside her keeper's house.

The roar of the trucks caused Coolidge to rub anxiously at her ankles. The peace of the high bluff overlooking the upper Chesapeake Bay was broken.

"Government orders," Annie said to Coolidge, and sighed. "There's a war on."

Now, here was the war at her door step. Once the trucks stopped, the Coast Guard troops piled out. She hadn't known quite what to expect, but not this. They looked like high school boys, not hardened troops.

The one exception was a man who might have been old enough to be their scoutmaster, or their father. He got out of a truck and approached, walking a bit stiffly from the long ride down the dirt road.

"Ma'am," he said, taking off his hat. She had seen newborn babes with more hair on their heads. He introduced himself as Thomas Heyward. "We're under orders to guard the lighthouse and secure this station against any enemy incursions."

"It's a lot of government foolishness, if you ask me," Annie said.

Heyward stiffened at that comment. "This lighthouse needs

protecting, ma'am. *You* need protecting."

"We'll see about that." Annie sniffed, sounding haughtier than she'd meant to. Tending the lighthouse on so many cold nights had left her with a permanently runny nose.

Heyward turned away without further comment and started shouting orders to the Coast Guard boys, leaving Annie feeling as if they'd gotten off on the wrong foot.

Just two days before, Annie had received word that her lighthouse—there was no way to think of it but as *hers*—had been deemed a strategic asset. One in need of military protection. She had been informed that a detachment of Coast Guardsmen would be sent to secure the lighthouse grounds for the duration of the war.

It all seemed more than a bit silly to Annie. The biggest threat she faced was the occasional fox or hawk that wanted to carry off one of her chickens. Now, the United States government was concerned that German U-boats might come up Chesapeake Bay to capture her lighthouse.

The situation would have made her late husband chuckle. As a lifelong lightkeeper, he had been well-used to the government's approach to management. He used to say, "Annie, rest assured that most government officials would rather shoot mosquitoes and swat elephants."

Annie was well aware that she had been the beneficiary of the government paying attention to details at times. It was President Coolidge who had signed a presidential order appointing her lightkeeper, overriding any objections about appointing a woman to the post. She had named her tomcat in his honor.

She also had to admit that the government had a point in claiming that Turkey Point Light was strategically important, located at the entrance to the Chesapeake & Delaware Canal. With the war, the canal had been particularly busy with ships carrying freight and personnel for the war effort. As part of the intracoastal waterway, the canal provided a route between the ports of Philadelphia, Baltimore, and Norfolk without having to enter the Atlantic, where U-boats did prowl. At night, people lined the beaches of Atlantic City and Cape May to gape in horror at the glow of burning ships far out at sea.

Annie watched the ships and tugs pass below, bound for distant ports or even for Europe, while she herself rarely left the lighthouse grounds.

Annie had become so self-sufficient that she almost took it for granted that there was a world beyond Turkey Point. Her world revolved around the 35-foot tall brick lighthouse built in 1833 by John Donahoo on a 100-foot bluff overlooking Chesapeake Bay. There were few spots so beautiful—or so remote. All the materials for the lighthouse and keeper's house had been brought in by boat.

The lighthouse was located at the end of a peninsula, and it was twelve miles up a dirt road through the woods to the town of North East. With the nearest telephone and store that far away, Annie grew most of her own food, keeping a garden and chickens. She caught rockfish whenever she wanted. A generator now provided electricity to operate the fog bell, but for more than a century the lightkeepers had been expected to ring it by hand throughout the night, which was an exhausting task.

Trying to ignore this new intrusion by the outside world to her secluded duty station, Annie went about her chores as usual, feeding the chickens, tending the vegetable patch, and lighting the lamp, of course. Meanwhile, the Coast Guard set up wall tents in the field near the lighthouse. They established what they called a "listening post" on the cliff. Sentries were posted and watches established.

The young Coast Guardsmen had a few single-shot Springfield carbines, left over from the Great War, that they had to share when on watch. She put more faith in the old double-barreled Iver Johnson shotgun she kept in the lighthouse to scare off the hawks and foxes. Annie was no military expert, but without so much as a machine gun or a mortar, she had to wonder just how much protection the Coasties were supposed to provide if German commandos stormed the beach.

The Coast Guard had its new listening post, but Annie had her own—a bench where she liked to sit on the bluff, looking toward the west. She and Mr. Poole sometimes went down there in the summer or fall, to have a mug of coffee after supper and watch a brilliant

Chesapeake Bay sunset.

This particular evening as she sat on the bench, there was no sunset to see, but only a fading of the daylight as the fog rolled in. What some might view as forlorn, Annie saw as a variation on a theme. She loved to watch the bay in all its seasons and moods.

On evenings like this, she missed Mr. Poole.

Mr. Poole had been several years older than Annie. In her mind, she still thought of him as *Mr. Poole*, although they had been equal partners as man and wife. On occasion, on nights that did not require one or both of them to tend the light or the bell, they made love in the creaky brass bed upstairs in the keeper's house, but it was a dutiful sort of lovemaking, each of them hoping to satisfy the needs of the other. They had found more satisfaction in a gentle companionship. They'd never had any children. Annie sometimes thought of the lighthouse itself as their child, because they had tended and loved it together, carrying out the countless chores from filling the lamp with oil to polishing the Fresnel lens to whitewashing the brick walls inside and out.

Mr. Poole had been a hard worker, busy from dawn to dusk and beyond, and he was also brave. She remembered how one night a vessel had foundered in a storm. She and Mr. Poole had made their way down the cliff path, lighting the way with a lantern, and peered out at the storm-tossed bay. The surface of the water, usually calm, roiled with whitecaps. They could hear the pitiful cries of men in the dark, but could not see the wreck.

Mr. Poole had taken a boat and rowed out. Annie was sure it was the last that she would ever see of him. But he had returned, ferrying a cargo of shivering survivors. Then he had turned the boat around and gone back for the rest of the crew. By some miracle, the little boat made it back with the remaining survivors before the wreck slipped beneath the waves.

The lighthouse service wanted to give Mr. Poole an award in front of Congress for saving those men, but he wanted no part of that. Instead, some official had driven the many dusty miles down to Turkey Point and presented the award to him. Mr. Poole chuckled that night as he put the framed certificate away in a drawer. "Just doing my job, Annie, and just doing what any decent man would do. Everyone can be brave when they need to be. There's no cause to give a man an award for that."

That was quite a speech, coming from the taciturn Mr. Poole. Annie agreed with what he'd said, but she was proud of him all the same. They had made love that night in the brass bed.

Mr. Poole had died too young, after catching a fever from being up all of a damp winter's night ringing the bell.

Sitting on the bench, she sipped her coffee and felt pleasantly alone, rather than lonely. The fog shifted in her direction, carrying the smell of salt and damp on the breeze.

What was that?

She thought that she heard a diesel engine in the growing dark, and then a shout or two in what did not sound like English. Annie leaned forward, straining her ears, but the fog and the slight breeze did not blow her way again.

Just before it was completely dark, Annie returned to the lighthouse and sought out Mr. Heyward to report what she had heard.

"I wouldn't worry about it," he said. "The boys at the listening post didn't report anything unusual."

"Maybe if they actually listened, instead of talking about baseball and girls, they might hear something."

"Mrs. Poole, are you telling me that you actually heard a U-boat out there?" Heyward could not quite hide his look of amusement.

"Well, I know that I heard *something*." She sniffed.

Heyward was a level-headed fellow, so he doubled the guard that night. He made the boys give him all their bullets, though, explaining that he didn't want them accidentally shooting any duck hunters or fishermen in the fog.

* * *

At the outset, the boys might have been disappointed that they weren't guarding some pretty young damsel in distress. She had a tower, but she was long past being Rapunzel.

Stuck in this remote duty, they made the best of it.

The Coasties had been sent to protect the lighthouse, but Annie soon found that she was the one protecting *them*.

She cooked up big pots of crab soup and made cornbread in her iron skillet, taking it all over to the lighthouse, which became a kind of gathering spot. On sunny days, the boys lounged on the grass in the shadow of the tower. She mended, tended to hurts and illnesses, and gave advice on broken hearts, or how to write a letter to a girl back home.

"Tell her how the blue sky over the water reminds you of her eyes."

"She has brown eyes, Mrs. Poole. Like leaf mush."

"For heaven's sake, don't write that! Just tell her that she has beautiful eyes."

"You reckon that's enough?"

Annie thought back to her own relationship with Mr. Poole. Sometimes the best compliment had been a simple one. "I reckon it is," she said.

She taught them the rudiments of tending the light, and of the lightkeeper's duties, though she wasn't about to relinquish any of them herself. She did have them carry up the heavy cans of kerosene to the top of the lighthouse, and showed them how to keep the lamp filled. She warned them away from the cliff's edges, which tended to crumble precipitously. She taught them how to ring the fog bell. The pendulum mechanism for the bell descended into a deep pit, so she dragged some boards across the open pit to keep any of the more careless young men from falling into it in the dark.

* * *

The Coasties had been there for six weeks when Mr. Heyward announced that he was taking all the boys for a night on the town.

"The boys are getting a little restless," he explained. "They need to blow off some steam."

Annie sniffed again, this time with genuine disapproval. She knew that "blowing off steam" was a euphemism for drinking beer in one of the roadhouses way up in Elkton, where there were likely to be loose young women from the munitions plants in town. Barefoot hillbilly girls, she had heard it whispered, had been bused in from mountain hollers down south to make bombs and artillery shells. Annie wondered what else those hillbilly girls might not be wearing.

Then again, she wasn't so naive that she didn't realize a young man needed something more entertaining than keeping watch over miles of empty bay and tending her vegetable garden. She worried about her boys, all the same.

"What about the Germans?" Annie asked. It had become something of a joke between them, since that night she had heard a diesel motor in the fog. There had been no further incidents, and the idea that a U-boat was going to anchor off the cliff and storm Turkey Point lighthouse now seemed ludicrous.

"I think the Germans will leave us alone for one night," Heyward said with a wink. He then added more seriously, "Besides, the weather is supposed to be clear as a bell. If they ever do attack, it's going to be on a foggy night when the spotter planes can't fly."

"Be careful up there in Elkton," she said.

"Aye aye." Heyward grinned. He seemed to be looking forward to getting away from the lighthouse for the night as much as anyone.

None of the young men wanted to be left out of the adventure, so it was decided that they should all go, it being unlikely that the Germans would pick that particular night to attack.

That was fine with Annie. She was used to being alone. In fact, she preferred it. But watching the two trucks drive off with the Coast Guard boys, it was the first time in years that she had felt lonely.

"I suppose it's just you and me," she said to Coolidge.

The cat rubbed contentedly against her ankles.

To keep that lonely feeling at bay, Annie kept busy. She was never one for sloth, but she doubled her efforts, pulling weeds in the vegetable patch, feeding her chickens, then finally climbing the narrow stairs of the lighthouse to give the Fresnel lens one last polish.

She stood back to admire her work. The lens was, in fact, more like a bejeweled sculpture in glass than a working maritime navigational aid. Its multiple layers and facets amplified the light almost magically, so that the beam reached for miles across the upper Chesapeake Bay.

Satisfied that not a single smudge marred the surface, Annie lit the lamp.

Soon after darkness fell, a heavy fog rolled in. The change in the weather was unexpected, but that was the Chesapeake Bay for you.

She looked down at Coolidge. "We'll be needing the fog bell tonight," she said to the cat. He followed her down to the bell, where she flipped the switch to start it.

Just before midnight, she went outside with Coolidge to check on the light. It seemed to be operating normally. But the fog bell had fallen silent. The bell was automated, driven by an electric motor run by the generator, and sometimes it stuck for one reason or another. Annie walked down to the bell and pulled back the boards covering the pit into which descended the two weighted chains that served as pendulums for the bell. Sure enough, with her flashlight, she could see that the chains had become entangled. She struggled to work them free.

In the quiet, she became aware of the sound of a diesel engine. Then a splash. Distinctly, she heard the sound of oars. Her ears strained to hear more. Then came the noise of a boat grinding ashore at the foot of the cliffs. Until that moment, she had been curious. Now, she was concerned. At her feet, Coolidge looked out into the darkness and yowled.

Annie was not sure what to do. Coolidge followed her down to the listening post—the one used by the Coast Guard, because it stood near where the trail led down the cliff to the beach. *Voices*. Surely, it couldn't be Germans coming up the cliff. It had to be duck hunters lost in the fog, or the crew of a broken-down vessel. Staring into the fog, she strained to see and hear.

Now, she heard footsteps. Stealthy ones. Slowly, the figures of several burly men came into sight, darker silhouettes against the backdrop of fog. She realized too late that her own silhouette was visible against the fog. The man in the lead froze as he caught sight of her. He turned and shouted something to the others.

Annie had still held out hope that she was being silly. This was all going to end with a laugh and offering a pot of coffee to some stranded duck hunters.

But the man's voice froze her with fear. He was speaking German.

Annie was still processing that fact when the German crouched and began to move toward her.

Annie snatched up the cat, and ran.

She knew that she could never outrun the commandos, much less a bullet. Fortunately, they hadn't started shooting; perhaps they still hoped for an element of surprise and wanted to take her alive. She glanced over her shoulder and saw two Germans close on her heels. They were going to catch her at any moment. She was a middle-aged woman, after all, and they were fit young men.

Annie swerved toward the bell pit. She knew just where it was in the dark, and leaped right across. Hard on her heels, the two Germans never saw the pit yawning in front of them. They fell 20 feet, screaming in terror, until they landed on the counterweights at the end of the chain pendulums, causing the fog bell to gong wildly. She snatched up the cat and ran for the lighthouse.

Annie wasn't sure how many more Germans were after her, but all that she could think to do was to reach the lighthouse. The light was like a beacon to her, the same way it had lighted the way for so many others on a dark night. The Germans must have slowed to see if they could help the broken men in the bell pit, because she managed to reach the lighthouse just ahead of them.

Annie didn't even have time to slam the door, and definitely no time to grab her old Iver Johnson shotgun and load it. She put down Coolidge and snatched up the first thing her hands touched, which was the cast iron skillet that she had used that morning to make a batch of corn bread. She swung it at the first commando who ducked his head through the doorway. The heavy skillet was made in Erie, Pennsylvania, by the Griswold Company, and weighed exactly four pounds. Joe Louis couldn't have delivered a harder knockout.

Dropping the skillet, she ran for the narrow stairs, with Coolidge leading the way. She had been up and down the lighthouse countless times so that her feet were quicker on the tricky, winding steps than the two clumsy Germans who came after her. But Annie soon reached the top of the stairway, and there was nowhere else to go but up the ladder into the cupola of the lighthouse. Once there, she turned and looked down at the two angry soldiers scowling up at her. Coolidge seemed to sense the danger, and caterwauled again. One man muttered something in German with a disgusted tone, and then started up the ladder.

Clutching Coolidge in her arms, Annie could only watch helplessly as the German ascended. What happened next was quite unexpected. One moment, Coolidge was hunkered in the crook of her elbow, and in the next, the tomcat had launched himself into the face of the German commando, claws extended. Coolidge stuck there like a burr.

The man howled, let go of the ladder, and hovered for a moment, arms pin wheeling. Then he plunged down the ladder and most of the way to the first turn in the winding stair, hit hard, and rolled down out of sight with Coolidge still clinging to him.

The remaining German stared into the wake of tangled tomcat and man, then looked up the ladder directly at Annie. He muttered what sounded like a curse and reached for his waist, where there was a gun in a holster. Annie closed her eyes, feeling awful about Coolidge, and knowing that this was the end.

But when there was no gunshot, she opened her eyes and saw that the German had drawn a knife instead, and was coming up the ladder. He had the knife clamped between his teeth like a pirate. The wicked, gleaming blade reflected the light from the lamp. Perhaps he felt the pistol would be too quick for the likes of Annie.

Desperate now, Annie picked up a jug of kerosene oil, used for fueling the lamp, and poured it over the commando.

Upon realizing that he was covered in kerosene, the German swiped at his face and muttered, "*Scheisse!*"

Their eyes locked across the short distance separating them. The German's pupils were black with anger. But the look in Annie's eyes caused the German to stop with just a few rungs of the ladder left to climb.

In her hand was a wooden matchstick. It did not seem like much of a weapon, compared to the commando's knife, but his eyes grew larger when she struck the match against the brick wall and it flared to life.

"That's for Coolidge," she said, and dropped the burning match down the hatch.

Fortunately for Annie, the saboteur's clothes did not explode. He caught fire more like a giant lamp wick. Even so, the flames were enough to send the man hustling down the stairway, screaming in panic. He ran outside and rolled on the dew-wet grass to snuff the flames.

What was left of the commando squad regrouped a hundred feet away. They had been trapped, battered with a skillet, clawed, and singed. It was time for a new plan of action.

Annie climbed down, having to clamber over the body of the German that Coolidge had attacked; he must have broken his neck in the fall. Coolidge was nowhere to be seen, and Annie felt a stab of grief. On the floor of the lighthouse lay the man she had hit with the skillet. Not only was he still not moving; he wasn't breathing, either. Fear must have given her more strength than she realized.

While the Germans deliberated what to do next, Annie took action and loaded her shotgun. She ran out after them, brandishing the double-barreled 12 gauge. She never would have admitted it later to anyone, being a little ashamed of the fact, but she screamed like a banshee wailing the rebel yell as she charged. Her keening howl of outrage sounded frightening even to her own ears.

Her battle cry lit the fuse of panic. What was left of the commando group turned and ran for their boat on the beach below.

Annie didn't bother to chase them down the trail. She dashed to the cliff's edge, and a minute later the fog parted just enough for her to spot the dark shape of a launch making its way out into the bay.

The German commandos were out of range by then, but that didn't stop Annie from letting them have it with both barrels.

* * *

That night, with their vision clouded by the fog and beer, the Coast Guard boys opted to camp on the dark and narrow dirt road. They arrived in the morning, cold and hung over. The sight that greeted them made them wonder if they might still be drunk. Two bodies lay in a neat line where Annie had dragged them. Broken and bloody, the corpses may as well have had X's over their eyes to show how obviously deceased they were, just like how dead men were depicted in the Sunday funnies.

Annie wasn't sure if she was more relieved to see the Coast Guardsmen or Coolidge, who showed up at first light, none the worse for wear.

She did, however, feel conflicting emotions about the dead men; it was not in her nature to harm anyone, even a German saboteur. She decided that she had only been defending herself—and the lighthouse—from attack.

Mr. Heyward expressed his astonishment, and then drove back to make a report. The nearest telephone was miles away at a Methodist church rectory. He returned with orders to bury the bodies in an unmarked grave, which they did. Everyone was sworn to secrecy. Heyward explained that the whole incident was to be hushed up to prevent public panic. Publicizing the fact that there were U-boats prowling Chesapeake Bay wasn't going to inspire confidence in the war effort.

The Coast Guard did not receive any reinforcements, and Heyward's superiors did not send the machine gun that he requested. Annie recalled Mr. Poole's words of wisdom about shooting mosquitoes and swatting elephants. All they got to defend Turkey Point Light was a box of hand grenades, which on the Fourth of July they had great fun hurling off the cliff. Everyone agreed that it was the best fireworks show they had seen in years.

To the boys' disappointment, they never did spot another U-boat.

Annie didn't mind.

David Hoffman

PLAYGROUND BULLIES, 1951

The ancient Ford school bus, "the cheese crate," rumbled along country roads, never exceeding forty miles an hour. There were frequent stops to pick up all the kids bound for Eastbrook's small white painted-brick elementary school.

It was September, 1951, and Ben Wald's family had just relocated from Manhattan to this quiet shoreline community on Long Island Sound. Ben, a small, docile nine-year-old with curly brown hair, clung to the rail of his seat as the rickety old bus bounced unmercifully over narrow winding roads. The roads transected pastures punctuated by stone walls and tranquil woodlands; farther along it went over narrow bridges and across tidal marshes that opened into rivers and streams that fed into the Sound. Ben's fleshy little face and hazel eyes betrayed a certain trepidation, if not alienation, as the rough and tumble country kids piled onto the bus. It was like being on another planet. Where, oh where, were those polite and well-groomed kids from Manhattan?

After his first day in the fourth grade, Ben burst through the doorway, "Mommy and Daddy, what do 'fuck' and 'shit' mean?"

Ben's father, Stanley, an aspiring young writer who taught at a local college, took a moment to reflect. "Benny, those are bad words that kids your age should not be using. Someday I'll explain it to you."

A few days later, Ben was seated on the homeward-bound bus next to Henry, unrefined and squarely built with conspicuously long dirty fingernails. Henry was sullen, but periodically seemed to relish tormenting kids he viewed as his inferiors.

At that moment Victor, an awkward boy with glasses, who exuded an odor of rancid bacon, boarded the bus. Victor took a seat near Ben as he swallowed some air and attempted a "H-hi, B-ben."

Henry immediately turned and poked Ben, saying, "OK, your turn to pick on Victor today!"

Ben looked at Henry in bewilderment, shaking his head.

Henry cast a look of disdain at Ben. "Yuh heard what I said!"

"Why should I pick on Victor?" Ben whispered meekly. "Victor never did anything to me."

This prompted a sharp jab to Ben's ribcage. Ben jerked around and tried to rub away the pain, but remained silent, ignoring Henry. In exasperation, Henry dug his long filthy thumbnail as deep as he could into Ben's soft fleshy forearm, leaving a visible trace of blood. Henry then turned away and reverted to his sullen mode for the rest of the ride.

Ben stifled his emotions until he stepped off the bus. Then he burst into tears. "Henry punched me on the school bus and scratched my arm because I didn't want to make fun of Victor."

Stanley Wald's eyes flashed in anger that quickly changed to sympathy, as he turned and whispered to his son, "We'll see what we can do about that."

But Alice, Ben's mom, shrieked in alarm, "Stanley, just look at his arm, it's punctured, I see blood, it might require stitches! We need to get him to Doctor Kaufman right away!"

Stanley remained calm as he inspected the superficial wound, vigorously wiping it with rubbing alcohol followed by iodine and a small Band-Aid.

Then, in an only slightly less agitated tone, Alice declared, "Stanley, we need to contact the school right away."

Because such incidents were seldom reported to authority figures in 1951, Stanley accordingly advised, "Tattletales are regarded as greater social pariahs than bullies. Tattletales get ostracized by classmates and get beaten up by bullies."

Alice countered, "Dr. Kaufman's wife warned me about the bullies in Eastbrook public schools. Why do you think they put little Barry into that private school across the river? We have plenty of money in your family trust fund, we can easily afford private school for Benny."

Stanley shot back, "Why do you think I put Ben into a public school in the first place? All my life I was sheltered by private schools. Just look at me now, the hothouse plant that I am!"

Alice knew it was true that Stanley often felt awkward if not intimidated when trying to communicate with average blue-collar guys. He wanted to see his young son develop into a more worldly man of tougher fiber than himself.

So Stanley's remedy for the situation was to fill a large empty feed sack with sand. The sandbag was then suspended by a rope from a sturdy limb of the tall oak that graced the Walds' front yard. The following day, as soon as Ben hopped off the bus, his father pointed to the sand bag. "Benny, just pretend that sandbag is Henry. Now, first a quick left jab to throw him off balance, and then follow through with a right as hard as you can. Pull those arms way back and give it all you can." Stanley coaxed and cheered Ben on to keep him pummeling the sand bag with his little fists again and again, until Ben could barely move his arms. Alice disapproved of the entire idea but didn't protest too vigorously as she watched Ben's progress.

After one week of this regimen, Ben meekly declared, "Daddy, I still don't think I could punch and hurt another kid, even if he was a bully." His exasperated father quietly excused himself and shuffled back into his small writer's den.

The following day, Ben arrived at school with a handsome pocket watch that his father had lent him to help track the time for a school event. Throughout the day Ben couldn't resist displaying the watch to his classmates. Billy Swenson, the mighty warlord of the playground, with strength and stature unrivalled among the other fourth graders, was quick to spot the watch. Billy was equally quick to propose a deal on the playground as a "fair trade." With the look of a determined Viking, he directed his steel-blue eyes down on small Ben, "Ben, that is a nice watch but I really need it more than you do. I have something even better for you that my father gave me." Billy pulled out a broken pen stamped with "Lazy Dog Tavern," a sleazy joint across the river that his father frequented.

Ben uttered a meek, "Thank you, Billy." Fear and the belief that maybe the pen was of some value prevailed as Ben handed over the watch. Ben was also awed by possessing something that had belonged to this much feared bully.

Later that day, Stanley became quite perturbed upon hearing the fate of his pocket watch. However, he soon conceded to Alice, "Well, it was only a watch, at least no further injuries."

The next day was a school holiday and pleasantly sunny. "Good day for a nice walk to the brook, Benny, and you'll feel better than yesterday," comforted Alice. Ben and his mother trudged along the meandering country road for almost a mile. Ben reached the brook first. The single-lane wooden bridge was situated below a scenic waterfall fed by an oval-shaped mill pond.

On the bridge stood stout Connie and her equally stout cousin Oliver, both dwarfing Ben. Connie lived across the road on a small dairy farm with her father, who had a reputation for unmercifully beating his cattle with a large club whenever they failed to move fast enough during herding. Connie had a reputation for being equally cruel, tormenting smaller kids on the playground by pulling or knocking them off swings and see-saws. Connie and Oliver had been fishing off the bridge using a bobby pin for a hook and stale bread for bait. Lying at their feet on the edge of the bridge was a hapless eel, struggling to get back into its aquatic environment.

Ben pitied the struggling eel. He glanced around quickly, and then a quick slide of his foot liberated the eel, sending it over the edge of the bridge back into its accustomed habitat.

Connie and her cousin spun around towards Ben with clenched fists, in a fury of disbelief, "Why did yuh put that eel back in the brook? Did yuh think it was poisonous?" Both of them backed off as soon as they saw Ben's mother round the bend in the road.

At school the following day, the class and the usual two attending teachers, Miss Portland and Mrs. Carlton, lined up for morning recess in the hallway that reeked of fresh paint and floor cleaner. Miss Portland was old and myopic, and once out the door, much preferred to remain stationary near the entrance. There she made a perfunctory effort to render supervision over some unsuspecting kid for a minor infraction. "Stop tossing sand on the hardtop," she would say, or she would offer a word of caution: "Your shoelaces are untied and you could trip."

Mrs. Carlton, considerably younger, was a more dominant force to be reckoned with. She had a fiery temperament and a reputation for smacking unruly boys with rulers and washing their mouths out with soap for uttering profanities. Foul-mouthed Billy was quite accustomed to being the recipient of her discipline.

While the students were getting in line, Mrs. Carlton slipped into the hallway bathroom for teachers. The bathroom was no bigger than a broom closet and the door was vented, unfortunately permitting both sounds and odors to become public. Billy and his followers, hearing the grunts from within, knew Mrs. Carlton would be occupied for some time. They gleefully welcomed the opportunity to rule the playground. Once Miss Portland swung the outside door open, the entire fourth grade made a mad dash out. Billy and his little gang quickly disappeared around the corner of the building in order to distance themselves from Miss Portland's favored roosting spot.

Today, Billy's gang included Mervin, his cowardly but devoted sidekick, Connie, Oliver, Henry, and a few other henchmen. Mervin was grinning like a Cheshire cat. In the presence of Billy, Mervin always exuded confidence. When alone, he was blandly passive. Other members of Billy's playground marauders were more fluid, varying from day to day. Some of them chose to be followers as an attempt to avoid becoming potential victims. However, that alone didn't guarantee them a safe haven. Depending on Billy's mood, one of these lesser followers might be randomly sacrificed as the victim of the day. A cry of "Let's get Donny today," or "Let's get Bobbie today," and all the remaining little marauders would eagerly follow Billy's command and storm after the unfortunate one, sometimes sending him fleeing to the white fence on the periphery of the playground. There he might bury his face in his sleeve to hide his tears. The humiliation was almost as hurtful as the pain of a few punches.

However, today the gang's immediate target was Ben. They

descended upon him with no mercy. "You threw our eel back! Your mommy ain't here to protect yuh today!" bellowed stout Connie and Oliver. With no further ado Ben received three solid punches in his stomach and a somewhat deflected but still painful punch on his right shoulder. He doubled over in pain and did his best to hold back a flood of tears and vomit. That satisfied the gang enough to move on. Besides, Miss Portland was just around the corner and had better hearing than eyesight. Ben suddenly began to experience a new feeling. Although both physically and emotionally hurt, he also felt anger swelling within him.

Not too far away was fat Freddy, a cousin of Billy's. Jaundiced looking and not a very bright light bulb, Freddy had a daily routine of playing with a jelly doughnut. The doughnut was oddly pear shaped, markedly similar to Freddy's own unique physique. As soon as recess began, out of the paper bag came the pear shaped snack, but it did not go directly into Freddy's mouth. Freddy tossed the doughnut up in the air four or five times, like a cat toying with a mouse. Each time, it landed on the hardtop. Finally, Freddy bowed over his prey, ready to grasp it with his teeth for the final kill.

Before he could open his mouth, the heel of Billy's hard leather boot squashed the jelly doughnut flat, grinding it into the hardtop, much like the demise of a plump toad on a country road. Freddy broke into a slow bawling sound at the loss of his much cherished snack as well as his favorite pastime. In spite of his limitations, Freddy had the sense not to challenge Billy. He knew only too well what a punch Billy could pack. Although they were cousins, it gave him little immunity.

Billy's gang continued on their course, circling around the playground. They sighted sweet but unkempt Irene standing alone. From an impoverished West Virginia mining town, Irene's family was not accustomed to hot running water. Only a hand pump served their shack on a back road in Eastbrook. Bathing for Irene was a rare event. As the gang approached, Connie blurted out, followed in sequence by Billy and then the others, "Hey Cootie-Cat, why are yuh afraid of soap and water? Why don't yuh ever take a bath? Why are your clothes so wrinkled? Yuh smell like a garbage can!" Then stout Connie scooped up a large handful of dirty sand off the playground and hurled it at Irene, splattering her face with dust, and saying, "Time for a dust bath just like our chickens." Irene looked down at the ground trying to hide her tears. Her only friend Dee-Dee, a year older and much bigger, came over to comfort her just as Billy's wicked little troop continued their course around the playground.

Leaning against the white schoolyard fence were the two freckled and toothy twins Earl and Albert. They were pressed against the fence as though they felt imprisoned in the playground and would much rather be somewhere else. Until a few years ago, they had lived in a remote Maine community where their father had been a struggling artist. Both brothers were incredibly shy, barely capable of uttering a word except to each other. Billy's gang cried, "Look at the two statues! Let's see if we can break them! Looks like they're glued to that fence!" Billy and Mervin vigorously pushed and punched Earl. Connie gave him a strong kick in the shin. Earl attempted to maintain his balance, but crashed to the ground. Before Earl could react, his brother Albert began crying; not because he was afraid, but out of pity for his much loved brother. This response satisfied Billy and his followers enough that they moved on across the playground.

They kept cruising around looking for other potential targets on the horizon, but no one was immediately apparent. Then suddenly Connie blurted out, "Hey! Let's go pick on Chicken Leg!" The others were quick to agree, "Yeh, let's get Chicken Leg!"

There on the far side of the playground stood Danny, with a steel brace on his leg, talking to little Sal. Danny's family were successful boat builders and worth a small fortune, but had no desire to send Danny off to a swank boarding school miles away. Slim and slightly above average height, Danny had a mop of red hair and a usually friendly smile in spite of having had polio. Only the steel brace on Danny's right leg, extending from ankle to knee, allowed him to maintain his balance and get around.

Little Sal stood half a head shorter than Danny; he had wavy black hair, olive skin, and dark eyes that looked about ready to pop out. Little Sal was endowed with terrific peripheral vision as well as a remarkable wiry strength and dexterity for a small boy. He and his immigrant family from Italy had once been with a travelling circus until his father had fallen from the trapeze. Little Sal was an adept juggler, leaving his audience spellbound during his performances. He was equally adept at balancing a long pole on his finger tip, bouncing it up and down without ever dropping it. In this waspish community, his small stature and Italian heritage earned him such playground monikers as "baby wop" or "little guinea rooster." However, his wit and physical agility usually kept the predators at bay. Both Ben and Danny admired little Sal's dexterity and there was a mutual feeling of respect among all three.

That morning Danny was occupied watching little Sal's juggling act which had now progressed from using two balls to three. With physical activities limited by his brace, Danny vicariously enjoyed watching the action of others. He loved the Arthur Godfrey show and would often recount what he had seen and heard the night before to little Sal, Ben, or anyone else willing to listen.

Billy's gang came charging into view from across the playground. On seeing Danny they shouted, "Look, there's Chicken Leg with his funny metal leg! Let's see if we can make him run!" None of them paid much attention to little Sal and his juggling act.

Danny did his best to ignore the cruel taunts of Billy, Connie, and Mervin. He continued to maintain his smile as he watched little Sal, mentally comparing him to someone he had seen on Arthur Godfrey the night before.

His lack of response only served to fuel the aggression of Billy and his followers. They increased the tempo of their taunts, "Run, Chicken Leg, run! Run, Chicken Leg, run!" and started grabbing at Danny. Danny's lack of response enraged Billy, who grabbed Danny firmly and flipped him hard onto the ground. At his orders, Mervin and Connie ripped off Danny's leg brace and tossed it away in the vicinity of little Sal. Then they started kicking grounded Danny and pummeling him, while shouting, "Now let's see if fucking Chicken Leg can run!"

Suddenly and unexpectedly, little Sal seized Danny's leg brace off the ground. Ever so quickly and deftly he wielded the brace with his right arm smack across the throat of Billy, who collapsed on the spot choking and spitting out some blood. The mighty warlord Billy burst into tears, bawling twice as loud as his many victims as he rolled on the ground rubbing his throat. Then, just as quickly with his left arm, little Sal swung the brace with a powerful sideways motion, catching Mervin in the groin. Mervin instantly crumpled forward, collapsing on the ground next to Billy. Mervin sobbed like a small girl who had just fallen off her first bicycle. Not wasting a second, little Sal somehow managed to swing his right foot upward in a lightning fast kick into stout Connie's rear end. Connie emitted a high pitched scream of pain as little Sal's pointed boot caught her on target. Connie tumbled forward and ran, shrieking in defeat and pain. It had all been so quick that the rest of Billy's little gang had not seen exactly what had happened, but the sound of the fearful screams and shrieks sent them scattering in all directions.

In less than a minute, little Sal had Danny's brace securely fastened back on his leg like nothing had ever happened. Then he and Danny were off around the corner, where little Sal calmly resumed his juggling act to the enjoyment of a new small audience. By this time, both teachers were sufficiently stirred by Billy's loud bawling to appear on the scene. Nobody, not even Billy, Mervin, or Connie seemed to know exactly what had happened. Nor did the teachers ever figure it out or bother to investigate it too thoroughly; they knew who the bullies were. Ben had quietly observed it all and stood in the background quietly smiling. Then he discreetly made his way across the playground to observe little Sal's juggling act.

When Ben climbed onto the school bus that afternoon he felt an inner glow as he reflected: "Maybe, just maybe, bullies deserve to get hurt sometimes."

Frank E Hopkins

RETURN FROM PARADISE

I fell in love twice on my first visit to the British Virgin Islands in February 2014. First, with the splendor of the green mountainous islands and friendly bays compared to the gray snow-covered flat landscape of Delaware. Then, with Emily Johnson, whose eyes were as blue as the tropical water and whose personality more pleasant than the steady refreshing trade winds propelling us on our excursion with the Delmarva Sailing Club.

Nothing can beat a tropical sail in the winter, especially when you are sending emails and pictures to your snowbound friends, co-workers, and relatives. We spent seven days sailing from island to island and anchoring in picturesque bays, eating at restaurants serving fresh caught seafood. The sailing trip started on Sunday morning, leaving the port of Road Town on Tortola Island. Joe, our skipper, instead of sailing the short distance directly to Cooper Island, allowed each sailor to take the wheel for forty-five minutes, sailing in the Sir Francis Drake Channel, to get used to the boat. Joe anchored the boat in Manchioneel Bay and we ate dinner at the Cooper Island Beach Club. The next day we spent three hours sailing to Maria Cay, a small four-acre island, located north of the eastern end of Tortola. Joe anchored in a shallow bay known for its scuba diving and snorkeling, less than a hundred yards west of Pusser's Marina Cay Resort, where we had dinner. The next day we headed northeast to Virgin Gorda, into twenty-knot winds that taxed our sailing skills. Joe controlled the helm and tacked into the wind with sails set at the first reefing point while we took pictures of the islands and sail boats near us.

Emily and I had known each other for a decade. We both attended DSC parties and dances, but we had never sailed on the same boat. When she stood next to me I saw the sunlight sparkle off the raven ponytail she wore when sailing. Her hair flowed loosely over her shoulder when partying, displaying her irresistible sex appeal. When we danced, I could see the top of her head at my eye level. I didn't know her age, and I wasn't about to ask, but I assumed she was at least five years younger than my fifty-six. Emily's excellent moves on the dance floor did not compare with her skill at the helm. Was she the first mate I had searched for since buying my boat fifteen years ago? Or were my thoughts clouded by the wine and rum we drank after anchoring for the day?

When we reached Virgin Gorda, we sailed north of the island, not tempted to enter the inlet's rock-studded shallows. Joe stayed at the helm until we were north of the Bitter End Marina before turning south, entering the bay through a narrow opening in the coral reef.

As we pulled into the Bitter End Marina, Paul, our oldest sailor, said. "I hope this isn't my last visit to the most entertaining marina in the Caribbean."

"Don't worry," Joe replied. "You've said that four times in the last ten years we've traveled here. Paul, I keep inviting you for insurance. While you're older, you're in better shape than any of us except Barbara. With you aboard I know the boat won't sink."

Never having sailed with this crew, their exchange impressed me, since I didn't want to drown.

After docking at 2:00 we broke out the beer, wine, and guide books to plan our two-day stay at this tropical paradise. None of us developed much of an itinerary for that day since the dinner dance for the nine DSC boats began at 7:00. The crew took naps on the boat or on the harbor beach.

Since this was my first Caribbean sail, the sight of the women I had only seen in shorts and tee-shirts, now dressed in light summer attire, confused me. I glanced from one to another trying not to blush and show my excitement. Women who had for years been buddies and sailing partners suddenly became desirable. There were so many, I had no idea what to do until Emily met us at the bar dressed in a turquoise wrap midi dress, which complemented her hair and blue eyes. She focused me.

The party space for our group consisted of tables for forty-eight situated close together in the restaurant for the buffet dinner. The Caribbean food of fish, seafood, Jamaican jerk chicken, barbeque pork and beef, and vegetables tasted great, and the wine flowed. No one left hungry. The band played melodic Caribbean music; however, the beat increased, and the lyrics became more sensual after 8:00 when the dancing started. The sailing club held our own against the other customers and after 10:00 we monopolized the floor. The dancers exchanged partners in the early evening. Couples formed after two hours. Emily became my partner until the music stopped at 11:00. Every one respected our space and none cut in. The crew returned to the boat, and since the five of us shared berths or slept on the deck, we never tried to consummate our relationship, although I couldn't stop thinking about her.

The next day our boat's crew and the other sailors split and pursued their own agendas. Our crew exchanged information on each one's plans. Barbara, our boat's leading aqua athlete, spent hours snorkeling. Paul walked around the expansive resort, reliving his earlier adventures. He planned to meet few sailors for a beer at the Crawl Pub, later in the afternoon. Joe, tired from herding his crew onto the boat, checking the provisioning before we sailed, and evaluating our sailing skills on the first two days of the trip, stayed on the boat sleeping or reading.

Emily and I took a cab to The Baths, carrying a beach blanket and a small canvas cooler containing our picnic lunch. The Baths contained lava columns rising out of the shallow water of the Sir Francis Drake Channel, evidence of the volcanic origins of Virgin Gorda.

After placing the blanket on the sand and anchoring its corners with our shoes and books, we disrobed to our bathing suits. While I have seen Emily in a halter and shorts before, this vision of her mentally and physically excited me and made me want to kiss her. Both of us put suntan lotion on. After Emily finished her legs and front, she handed me the lotion and said, "Please do my back."

With a smile, I gladly obliged. When she noticed my over-enthusiasm, she said, "Turn around and I'll do yours." Her hands lingered on my shoulders, when suddenly she removed them and said, "That's enough lotion for now."

I pondered, fantasizing what "now" meant.

We swam and stayed in the water until 1:00. After sitting on the blanket, Emily said "Let's eat." She took out the chilled bottle of Chardonnay, two plastic glasses, and a corkscrew and handed them to me. Without exchanging words I opened the wine, poured it into the glasses, recapped the bottle, and placed it in the cooler. Emily placed pieces of jerk chicken on two plastic plates set in front of us, opened a bag of potato chips, and placed it between us.

While eating she discussed her marriage and divorce, and I reciprocated with the personal history of my ex-marriage and the long search for a mate. This was our first serious conversation about each other's heartbreaks and desire for a more stable, permanent relationship. My interpretation of where we were headed differed from hers, as I found out when I leaned over to kiss her. She reached out and tenderly caressed my face with her hand as she pushed it aside so my well-aimed kiss only touched air a few inches from her face.

"Let's wait till later when we're in private. Someone from another boat could see us and start rumors that could embarrass us and stop our relationship from developing."

"Sorry, it seemed like the correct time for me. You're right." No one had ever rejected me with such warmth and promise as she had.

After sunbathing we caught a cab back to the Bitter End. We saw Barbara sitting in the boat's cockpit sipping a coke when we returned.

"Did you enjoy the snorkeling?" Emily asked.

"Loved it until I saw a shadow pass over me. Looking up, I watched a giant grouper, four times my weight, with a mouth twice the width of my hips pass overhead. Scared, but without panicking, I let the fish continue and quietly swam underwater to shore and left the water. I won't go back."

"Thank God, we didn't experience anything like that at The Baths," Emily responded.

Strange for me, but our conversation became warmer and friendlier on the ride back, at dinner, and when we parted for the evening. Emily gave my hand a warm squeeze and planted a kiss on my cheek as we retired to our bunks. My passion cooled, and I thought or hoped we had an unspoken agreement to develop our relationship.

The next morning we raised the anchor and left the marina through the narrow break of the bay. We set sail on a southwest course to Norman Island, at twenty-eight nautical miles the longest leg of the cruise. The prevailing northeast winds powered our boat, so we arrived at the Bight, a bay on the western side of Norman Island, early enough to claim one of the scarce mooring buoys. While still early we drank the obligatory beer or wine after the sail ended. Since we had eaten lunch hours earlier we motored ashore on the rubber dingy and explored the island. Barbara declined to wear her bikini, still afraid, while everyone else wore their bathing suits under their shorts and tee-shirts.

After we tied up the dingy and stood on firm ground, Joe said, "Let's meet back here at six. We have to decide where to eat. We can eat here at the Pirate's Bight, a quiet family restaurant, or motor over to Willie T's, the ninety-eight foot schooner-converted-restaurant offshore. Willie T's DJ plays loud rock-and-roll and it's the place to go if you want to dance and meet someone. We can always eat here and drink at Willie T's later."

Paul answered first, "Let's eat here. You kids can go dancing, but drop me off at the boat first."

Barbara said, "I'm with Paul. Eat here and take me to the boat. I have a boyfriend in Baltimore."

Emily looked at me and answered for us, "I'm with them. We need to wake up early to get a mooring at Foxy's. I don't want to stay out late."

Joe said, "Tony, unless you want to stop at Willie T's, let's make it an early night. You know I have a girlfriend in Washington and don't want any stories getting back to her."

"Agree. Let's motor to the boat after dinner." I blushed as I saw Emily smile at my answer. Having heard of the good times at Willie T's before the trip, the group's decision disappointed me, but Emily's smile made me realize I made the right decision.

The crew split up to explore the island, except for Emily and me. She carried a flashlight and led me to the caves, a prime tourist location. After we left and didn't see any of our crew Emily took my hand. An exciting and flattering event I expected would be the first of many.

Joe raised the anchor before 8:00, steered the boat for Jost Van Dyke Island, and sailed past "The Indians," four rock pinnacles thrusting fifty feet above the waves. At least ten boats had dropped anchor there, with their crew enjoying snorkeling around the rocks. We sailed through the strait between the western edge of Tortola and the small Great Thatch Island. Only three mooring buoys remained when we arrived after noon. Emily said, "Don't stuff yourself at lunch. You'll need an empty stomach to appreciate the barbeque at Foxy's."

"Is it all you can eat?" I asked.

"No, you can only go through the food line once, but the waiters encourage each diner to fill their plates as high as possible," Emily replied. "The food is great, but I recommend skipping the bread, salads, and vegetables and concentrating on the seafood, fish, and beef."

Most of us already practiced this philosophy on our many sailing trips.

"It's our last group party and dance, so enjoy the food and the sail, since in two days we return from paradise to the frigid Middle Atlantic states," I said.

"Weather.com forecasts heavy snow storms for the East this

weekend, at least a foot in New York, Philly, Baltimore, and DC, with temperatures in the low twenties, so have a good time tonight," Barbara said.

We listened to her, but it didn't douse our enthusiasm. After a light lunch we went snorkeling over the coral reefs near shore, trying to avoid the diving pelicans as we swam.

The evening at Foxy's exceeded our expectations, and the food was as great as Emily promised. The music was easy to dance to and included many of the songs written by the former owner, Foxy, now deceased. Emily and I spent the evening dancing together with no one else asking us to dance, an unlikely event at a DSC party. Noticing the sly smiles our friends directed at us, I realized the club members had already designated us a couple. I wasn't so sure unless Emily and I confirmed it after the sail. I felt as if I was in high school again.

The boat rental company required us to return to Road Town by 5:00 p.m. on the last day of the trip so the marina staff could check the boat to make sure we hadn't damaged it. Joe raised the anchor late in the morning after we slept off our excess food, alcohol, and dancing, and sailed at a slow relaxed speed. Even so we arrived an hour early.

The crew walked to the marina bar to meet our sailing friends to talk about our great adventure and to invite everyone to our boat for wine and cheese at 6:00. The other sailors said they would bring their leftovers. Since we couldn't take the alcohol or food back to the US, we tried to consume as much as possible that night. The flat screen above the bar showed a weather map of the eastern US being inundated by snow for Sunday night. We consumed all the food and drinks except tomorrow's breakfast, which Joe told us not to bring topside. Emily hid two slices of rye bread, a breast of jerk chicken, and Dijon mustard.

Since we had to leave the boat by 9:00 we arose early, ate breakfast, stowed the garbage in large plastic bags, and carried them to the end of the pier. While we were cleaning up the boat, Joe said, "Emily, what are you doing?"

"Making a chicken sandwich for lunch."

"You can't bring that past US customs."

"We'll see."

"Tony, talk sense into her."

"She can do what she wants." I guess I said the right words since her scowl at Joe turned into a smile after I spoke.

"We won't post bail if they arrest you," Joe said.

"Don't worry, Joe. Once we're off the boat, you're not the skipper anymore."

Harsh words. Do I have to worry about her tongue in our future?

We left the boat before the deadline and took the marina shuttle to the ferry slip. The passage through British Customs was pleasant and uneventful. They didn't ask us if we were taking food out of the BVI.

US Customs wasn't as pleasant. The ferry to Charlotte Amalie on St. Thomas carried over a hundred people. As we debarked from the boat, we saw a line at least fifty yards long with people waiting to get into the customs building. Thirty minutes passed before we could enter to discover another long line leading to the customs portals. As we got closer, we noticed only four of the portals out of the ten had customs officials processing entrants. This led to loud complaining.

One security guard gave us an explanation, "The Federal budget deal where Congress has frozen all expenses for most federal agencies causes this congestion. Get mad at Congress. Customs staff don't like it, either."

While this didn't make us happy, we moved at a slow pace until we reached the customs inspector. Emily walked ahead of me. I couldn't hear their conversation, but felt sorry for her when she handed him her backpack. I moved in closer since I didn't want to miss Emily being apprehended.

In less than ten seconds he pulled out the bag with the chicken sandwich. "I thought you said you had no food."

"I planned to eat it at the airport. It wouldn't have gotten into the US."

"Lady, you are in the US. I have to confiscate it or you'll have to eat it."

"I'll eat it."

He gave her the sandwich, "Stand over there and return when you're finished."

Poor Emily, having to eat a dry sandwich with nothing to drink. I tried to remain stoic as the customs agent took my passport. But I looked back and smiled, and she returned an icy stare.

Joe, Paul, and Barbara waited for me in the lounge.

"Where is Emily?" Joe asked.

"She's eating her chicken sandwich."

The three laughed, and I joined in, hoping Emily would never learn of their response.

"We're getting worried. Customs has taken so long we're afraid we might miss our planes," Joe said.

"Take a taxi. We'll meet you there. I'm sure Emily would be more comfortable not riding in a small cab with you," I said.

Everyone laughed again.

Emily passed customs within ten minutes after the others left. I explained why we were alone and Emily smiled.

The scene at the small Harry Truman Airport shocked us. Lines for all the airlines filled the ticket counter lobby. As I walked by the arrival and departure screens, I saw numerous departures to mid-western cities canceled. Our flight to Philly had an on-time status. We stood on line forty-five minutes to get our boarding passes.

Emily and I walked to the departure gate to wait the thirty minutes before our plane boarded. I walked over to Joe and Barbara, who sat stone-faced, not talking.

Emily stayed behind, saying, "I'll hold our seats. It's crowded here." I thought she wanted to avoid any comments from the crew about being stopped by US Customs.

"Hi, didn't you have an early departure?" I asked.

Joe answered, "We did. But all flights into Charlotte, North Carolina, have been canceled. We're flying to Miami this afternoon. If Dulles airport is open tomorrow; they'll take-off. If not, we have to wait another day."

"What happened to Paul?"

"He left an hour ago. His plane goes through Atlanta to get to DC National Airport, which is still open. Paul might be okay."

"Good luck. I have to get back since we're boarding soon."

I told Emily what had happened. She seemed nervous.

We boarded the plane and had an uneventful flight, with warm romantic conversation discussing our plans for the next weekend.

After we landed, I looked at the departure screen and said, "They closed BWI and National."

"Since Paul left earlier, he might have made it home," Emily said.

"You were supposed to fly from Philly to National. How will you get home?"

"I don't know. Either by train or an airport shuttle."

"The train and roads may be closed and a shuttle won't get through. Change your flight to Salisbury and you can stay with me in Ocean View."

"Thanks for the offer, but I have an important meeting at work on Monday that I can't miss."

"You might be stranded here all night. The offer is still open," I said with a smile.

Emily replied, "We have to know each other better before I spend the night with you."

"I have five bedrooms. You can sleep on the second floor."

"Sounds good. But I can't get stuck in Delaware. I have to prepare for Monday's meeting tomorrow and my PC is at home," she said smiling.

With that she got her luggage and kissed me goodbye.

The commuter flight to Salisbury was the last flight out of the Philly airport, as they closed it a few minutes after we departed. The pilot announced the closure as soon as the plane leveled off. The swirling snow surrounded our plane for the rest of the short flight.

When I entered the Salisbury Airport baggage area, I turned on my cell phone and noticed a message from Barbara. "Read the Philly airport closed. Are you two okay?"

I called her back, "The plane landed before the airport closed. I caught the last plane out to Salisbury."

"Let me speak to Emily."

"She's not with me."

"I thought you two lovebirds were inseparable."

"Not quite. She left me."

"Don't worry. You'll see her again."

I changed the subject and asked, "Will you and Joe be able to get home tomorrow?"

"Yes, we fly out tomorrow morning at nine. Paul called me and said he's stuck in Atlanta. They closed the airport a half-hour after he arrived."

I woke up the next day thankful, that unlike my friends, I was home. I looked forward to the after-BVI-sailing party in a month when everyone could tell of their hardship arriving home. Rather than gripe, they would probably laugh at their misfortune. As my custom, I walked into the kitchen, turned on the coffee, and went to the study to open my email.

The first email I decided to open had the title *Never Again* and the sender Emily Johnson.

Hi Tony,

Never again will I return from a Caribbean sail and fly into a Northeaster dumping over a foot of snow swirled around by gale-force winds so no one can see more than three car lengths ahead. Since the snow had closed Amtrak, I had to share a cab with three other sailors, costing $125 each to drop us at separate locations in Montgomery County. It took three hours for a normal forty-five drive and we passed six accidents. Next trip, when it snows, I'll either stay an extra day and let the storm clear out, or if you forgive my stubbornness for the delay at Customs and for leaving you at the airport, I'll fly with you to Salisbury and enjoy a nice warm bed in Ocean View.

Your future sailing first mate (if you'll have me),

Emily.

I sighed and smiled!

Brent Lewis

CHURN CREEK 1964

Ketchum Bailey sat on the ground above a sliver of pebbled beach, his bare feet at the edge of the chill, shallow water. His secondhand bicycle rested on its kickstand near a patch of budding bulrush and cattail, a white rubber work boot sheathing each handlebar.

He heard Mary's Pontiac arrive at the head of the trail and regretted not waiting to walk with her. It took her a few minutes to make her way through the footpath's thorny overgrowth to the small tidal pond that they, since childhood, along with Ketch's sister Dubois, always considered their secret spot. They used to catch minnows here in summer, ice skate here in winter, and they never found a better spot to play hide-and-go-seek.

Fifteen years had passed since they'd last been to Churn Creek Cove together. In the cultural wake of Elvis, Martin Luther King, and JFK, the world had harvested bushels of change, but both Ketch and Mary knew that the Chesapeake Bay's rural Eastern Shore was still no place for a black man to get caught with a married white woman.

"Looks like nobody's been back here for a while," Mary said, approaching from behind, playing like she'd snuck up on him.

Ketch turned a degree, peered over his shoulder at her and grinned. Mary, curvy and strawberry-blonde, her smile as soft as ever, wore blue canvas boat shoes, a plain yellow dress, and sunglasses pushed to her freckled forehead. Ketch could see her eyes. Her eyes changed colors all the time. Today they were more gray than green.

"I think the Elberms, Royal and Roy, gig frog in here sometimes,"

Ketch answered, rising to greet her. "I know they set a mess of muskrat traps over in that far marsh every winter, then go around saying they better not catch nobody trespassing." Ketch chuckled at such bare-assed foolishness. "And they don't even own the property."

Mary grasped both of Ketch's hands and held them to her chest a moment. "Hey, Ketch, honey," she said with her natural guarded warmth and a hug. "I've missed you. It's been too long." She fidgeted with her oversized knit handbag. "Have you had lunch? I grabbed subs and beers from the walk-in."

Mary settled into a crook of the ancient sycamore they called Audrey Hepburn for her two knobby-kneed roots protruding from the cove's southern bank. Audrey stretched a hundred feet into the sky and must have been twice as old. "Thanks for coming," Mary said to Ketch.

"Not a hard go," Ketch replied. "End of oyster season and crabs haven't come on yet. Packing house is slow. Only had half a day today."

"You all have a nice Easter?"

"Real nice. The cousins came down from Baltimore. Dubois enjoyed playing rummy with Mom-Mom and the older folks."

Ketch withdrew the red plastic sword from his sandwich's white paper wrapping and unrolled lunch. He hadn't realized how hungry he was until his first bite. Klegg's pool hall made the best cold-cuts. Ketch liked his with extra cheese, mayonnaise, and hot peppers. Tasted like having a choice.

He got two chews in before Mary, her own sub still on her lap, freed but unbitten, tried to ruin it for him. She hadn't even given him a chance to pop his can of Schlitz.

"I can't take it anymore," said Mary. "Let's do it. Leave. You and me and your sister. Let's go. Let's get away from here."

* * *

Ketch waited until he heard Mary drive off before he slipped his boots back on and started home.

Cresting the incline where the cove's path meets Possum Farm Road, he glanced to his right and saw, parked in the roadside gravel a quarter mile away, a pickup truck that he recognized.

Ketch pointed his bike in the opposite direction.

He hoped the truck's occupants had not seen Mary leaving their meeting place. Mary's reputation was already soaked-through bad enough.

The truck, a canned-pea colored 1956 Studebaker, inched behind him with an unhealthy rattle deep inside its machinery. Ketch looked over as Royal and Roy Elberm pulled next to him. Royal drove, his face resembling an overstuffed cherry pie. Skinny-ass Roy sat in the passenger seat taking a slug from a pint of bottom-shelf Canadian whiskey. Ketch gave them a nod, then faced front and pedaled with no adjustment in speed, steady as she goes.

Royal Elberm, loud enough to be heard over his ride's clatter, said, "Wha'chasay, Sidney Poitier?" By the look on his mug, Ketch could tell Royal was somewhat surprised by his own rhyme.

"Not much, Royal. How you all doing?"

"Oh, we doing fine," Royal said. "Just having us a little lunch." He held the bottle now, laughing as he hoisted it. "You want a drink, Ketchum?"

"No, thank you," Ketch said. "Headed to see my aunt and uncle. You know I'd hear about it if I came in there with hooch on my breath."

"That's sure right," Royal sneered, then shot Ketch a shit-eating grin. "Why'nt you throw your ol' bicycle in back? Me and Roy'll give you a ride."

"No thank you. I need the exercise."

Royal steered with his left hand draped over the top of the wheel, a cheap stogie burning down to his tarred knuckles. He stared ahead for an eternal minute, then took a swig and handed the bottle back to Roy. He said, "I 'spect you getting all the exercise you can handle, Mr. Poitier."

Ketch said nothing.

Royal coasted along. "We going by Klegg's. Sure you don't want a ride?"

"I haven't been in Klegg's for years."

Royal cackled with a high pitched hee hee. "Hear that Roy, said he ain't been in no Klegg's. For years. What you think about that?"

Roy leaned over to look past his rotund cousin. He hollered through buckteeth, "He's lying. Ain't none of 'em stay out of no place they want to go no more."

Roy and Royal laughed.

Ketch said, "Ya'll need to go on to wherever you're headed, stop yakking your mess to people."

Royal made a pouty Jerry Lewis face. "Just trying to look out for you, boy."

"Well, thanks again," Ketch said, and waved them off.

Ketch and Royal gave each other the eye for a few beats. Then Royal blew him a Hollywood kiss and hit the gas, raising a squall of chips and white dust from the road's crushed oyster shell surface.

* * *

Mary went home. Not back to where she'd grown up, not the place that still felt like where she should go when she said she was going home, but to her husband's house. The house he chose when Mary got pregnant, the house he bought with a loan secured by his parents; the house they moved into the night they got hitched. The house that spoke all of Wesley Walter, WW to his friends, and almost nothing of Mary.

She made instant coffee from hot tap water and lit a Chesterfield. She sat in the chair she always sat in at the scarred Formica-topped kitchen table they never got around to replacing.

Their son was at school and Wesley was out, supposedly getting his workboat, a 36-foot deadrise tuck stern named the *Mary Annie*, ready for crabbing season. More likely he'd spent most of his day bullshitting with the other watermen docked near him, including his father and brother. Those bayfaring ol' buzzards gossiped more than a beauty shop peanut gallery.

The crabbing was predicted to be good this year. Mary hoped so for all concerned. Winter had been rough. The Narrows froze twice and nobody worked for weeks. A lot of watermen, including Wesley, accepted handouts. Their families might've starved if they hadn't. Watermen think of themselves as independent, nobody-tells-me-what-to-do types. Every government voucher was a gut punch.

Making a reliable dollar on the water seemed to be getting next to impossible. Since Wesley didn't know how to do anything but fish the Chesapeake, his family's survival would forever depend on the catch of the day. Like many in his calling, Wesley Walter kept zero savings, not dime one.

Mary still helped at her parents' pool hall two or three days a week. Wesley grumbled enough to let her know he didn't much care for her spending any more time there than that.

Klegg's was a fixture in the county a decade before Mary, Norman and Alice's late-life and unexpected only child, was born. In a region tense with racial division, and with most local businesses catering to a white clientele, owning the lone bar where black men could drink beer and shoot pool without harassment had proven to be, plain and simple, a low-profile gold-mine.

Mary's parents were known to treat their clientele with fairness, but both elder Kleggs were well aware that the impending end of legal segregation would undermine their livelihood. Her father was taking history's flow personal. A meaner side of him, a side Mary didn't often see before, started making routine appearances. Her parents, like her husband, ran a tight ship getting tighter. These days, no misconduct was tolerated at Kleggs' pool hall.

Mary finished her cigarette. Wesley wanted things she couldn't bring herself to give him. If she were ever going to escape, it would have to be soon.

* * *

On the Friday after Mother's Day, Wesley Walter came home drunk.

Crab season did not start well.

"Where's Tooey?" Wesley asked his wife.

Mary sat at the kitchen table playing out a busted hand of Solitaire. Wesley rummaged through the refrigerator. He peeked inside the freezer section. The door wouldn't close tight because of all the frost.

There was nothing inside but four metal ice trays and a half eaten grape Popsicle. He grabbed another bottle of beer instead.

"He wanted to stay with your mom and dad again," Mary said.

"They *are* the grandparents what care for him, y'know."

She changed the subject. "I didn't expect you so early. I was planning on making meatloaf for dinner. If you're hungry, though, I can fry some hamburgers. There's leftover coleslaw, and chips in the cupboard."

"I'm good." Slouching against the counter, he raised his Pabst Blue Ribbon in a silent toast. "What've you been doing today? Wifey?"

She thought that maybe the sheets drying on the line outside and the piles of folded clothing throughout the house might have provided a clue.

"Laundry," she answered. "I cleaned the bathroom. Tooey forgot his lunch so I drove it over to him."

"My mom could have done that. She works right across the street."

They both lit cigarettes.

"He called me. No sense bothering Ruth. His lunch was all bagged and sitting right here." She handed him their Enchanted Forest souvenir ashtray. "I saw his teacher for a minute."

"Yeah?"

"Yeah." Mary was determined to not let him push her into an argument. "She said he's doing well. She's concerned he might not socialize with the other kids enough, but she thinks he'll bloom next year."

"Tooey's a good boy." Wesley inhaled deep, then pivoted to blow smoke through the open slats of a jalousie window.

"Yes, he is," she agreed.

"So why are you doing what you're doing to him?'

Mary dropped a seven card into her waste pile.

"What am I doing to him?"

"Running Ketchum Bailey."

Mary took a puff and focused on Wesley, trying not to show how surprised she was. "Why in the world would you say something like that?"

"Well, you are, aren't you?"

"No," she said. "Of course not."

"Don't lie to me," he said. "Ain't like you don't have it in you."

She scowled. "What's that supposed to mean?

"You know damn right well." He stubbed the Camel out with his thumb. "When we got married, you know what I dealt with, and now there's talk again. People saying."

"Who? Saying what?" She hated 'people saying'.

"Just people." He was smug. "You been to Churn Creek Cove lately?"

Again, stunned. "No. Why would I go there?"

He finished his beer, looked like he was thinking about cracking another. Mary stood. "Let me make us something to eat."

He grabbed her wrist. Not hard, and he let go before she could turn on him, but he grabbed it. He said, "I told you, I'm good," and then stood there mirroring her glare.

As she marched away, he asked, "Why ain't we had no more babies?"

He'd dug up a bone of contention they'd been gnawing on for a long time.

She stayed on course. She snatched a pile of their son's underclothes from the sofa and slammed them into their designated bedroom drawers. She took deep breaths and tried to keep her distance from Wesley, but he tired of waiting and followed her as she walked from Tooey's room into their own.

"I been trying to get you pregnant since Tooey started kindergarten. Now I'm glad ain't nothing took hold."

Mary edged him aside, stepped to the closet for hangers.

"It'd be a damned shame," he continued, "to put another kid through having you for a mother. Even if you weren't going around with Ketchum Bailey, you bring trouble by just being."

She faced him. Tears welled but didn't spill over. "Being what?"

"Being what you are, a ni-"

"Don't say what you think you want to say," she told him.

He in his stocking feet, she in loafers, they stood eye to eye. She said, "I haven't gotten pregnant because I always use a diaphragm. Always. Every time."

"Why would you deny me more kids?" he growled.

"Because you knew, from the beginning, that this was one big mistake. A mistake that keeps getting worse."

He dogged her all the way back to the kitchen. She went to the sink and he to the back screened door. He stopped to put on his boots.

"You know," he said, "I stomached all that crap everybody put me through, because I had faith in you. I had faith you could be a good person and do right. But I see now I can't never trust you, and you are always going to be what you are."

"I don't see how anybody could ever be anything but that," she said.

* * *

The tide was coming in and the bay grasses were thick. Ketch, standing, paddled a flat-bottomed rowboat out from the county landing to the deeper water where his Uncle Nut kept the *Sue Ellen,* an old-fashioned log canoe converted to accommodate an inboard engine. She was tied to a skinny pole hand-driven into the creek's muddy bottom.

The day before, Nut had changed the boat's water pump, but ended up with a leak that wouldn't quit. He asked Ketch to take a look. Ketch found that his uncle hadn't clamped the hoses hard enough, so after an easy fix, he checked every connection onboard from mechanical to electrical.

At eighty-six, Nut Bailey's body was hobbled from a lifetime of oystering and hauling crab pots. He couldn't twist a screwdriver like he used to, but his mind was sharp and his will to make a living steadfast. Working the water was the one place colored men held equal footing with their white competitors.

Ketch wasn't much for it. He'd gotten a job at the seafood packing house as a kid and stuck there until these days he pretty much ran Rio Wilmur's business. He'd learned all kinds of trades and expertise at Wilmur's side. Ketch could do almost anything.

Rowing back to shore, Ketch noticed a scant leak at the skiff's stern. He made a mental note to return and seal it for Nut his next chance.

It had been a drizzly day, but the sun crept out from behind the clouds late that afternoon. The creosote smelled fresh around the bulkhead. Ketch sat on the warm aluminum of a piling cap. He plucked his spiral notebook from his back pocket and was double checking Wilmur's numbers for the day when he heard a distant vehicle, the first since he'd gotten there, headed in his direction.

He'd ridden his bike from work that afternoon and his sister was supposed to pick him up here when she finished her kitchen-prep shift at the restaurant.

From its knocking emissions, Ketch didn't have to wait until the truck came into view to know it wasn't Dubois arriving in her well-tuned, two-door Ford.

Royal Elberm cut his engine. "Howzit hanging, Mr. Poitier?"

"It's all right."

"Lots of bad talk going around," said Royal. "Me and Roy been worried about you." Roy leaned over to wave, a redneck Alfred E. Neuman.

"Well, I appreciate it," Ketch said. "But maybe you two need to stop worrying with everybody else and worry about yourselves a while."

"Some people," Royal said, "would take that as a threat."

"Ain't no threat. I just know y'all been spreading bullshit."

"It ain't no bull. You know what me and Roy seen." Royal scratched inside his ear and inspected his finger.

Ketch stood. "I know what you believe you saw."

Roy Elberm slid out of the other side of the truck, took a protracted draw off his cigarette, and flicked it away.

Royal said, "WW wants a talk with you. He's right up the road at the Towed Inn."

Roy stepped around the rear of the truck. He held a shotgun.

"So Roy'll keep you company while I run and get WW," Royal said. "Don't let him start nothing, Roy. Ketchum comes at you, shoot him and say he jumped you. Say you was back here hunting spring turkey out of them woods over there."

"How do I say I got here?" Roy wanted to know. "Ketchum has his bicycle, that 'splains him. I live seven miles that way. What am I doin' way over here huntin' turkeys, Royal? How. Did. I. Get. Here?"

Royal shook his head, "I don't know. Tell 'em you swum. Don't shoot him and there ain't nothing to worry about." Royal looked Ketch in the eye. "I'm gonna trust you to not let him do nothing stupid," he said, pointing at Roy and starting the Studebaker.

"Roy," Royal yelled over the ding-ding-dinging of his truck, "I'll be five minutes." He shifted into first and reconsidered. "Maybe ten," he said. "Don't do nothing stupid for ten, fifteen minutes."

"I won't," said Roy as his cousin sped off.

"Don't you shoot me," Ketch said.

"Don't give me no reason."

Roy went into his shirt pocket. He one-handed a Lucky Strike and struck a match without removing it from its pad. Ketch shifted his weight and Roy flinched, saying, "Don't make no sudden moves."

"I'm taking a step back, that's all," Ketch said. "Why would you and Royal start trouble with me and WW, Roy? There's nothing between Mary and me."

"We seent you at Churn Creek."

"You didn't see nothing. I rode back there to sit by the pond a spell," Ketch said, lolling against the piling, "and here she comes. She saw me and left, never said a single word to me. You had to have seen her drive in and then drive right back out."

"No, we did not," Roy said between drags. "We got there as she left the cove. Who knows how long y'all was back there."

"You know I don't mess around where I don't belong."

"I know I don't buy none of your shuck and jive, Ketchum Bailey," said Roy. "And Mary Klegg always did like dark meat."

Ketch squinted at his uncle's skiff. "Damn."

"What's wrong?" Roy asked.

"Nut's rowboat's leaking," Ketch said. "You mind if I get down there and stuff a rag in that? Might keep her from sinking until somebody puts some caulk around there."

Roy looked dubious.

"No matter what," said Ketch, "I don't see no sense letting Nut's skiff sink on him. Hell, you want, why don't you climb aboard and fix her yourself."

Roy stepped back, "You do think I'm simple. No, you just go ahead."

Ketch stepped into the boat, extracted his handkerchief from his hip pocket; touched his penknife. He knelt on the bottom boards and stuffed the cloth into the split. Roy hovered above and said, "That ain't fixin' nothin'."

"You're right," said Ketch. "Hand me your caulking gun."

"Yeah, ha-ha, funny. You won't be such a smart aleck when Royal comes back with WW and who knows who else. Might be a few fellas sitting around the Towed looking for something to do this afternoon."

Ketch used the oar to steady himself as he stood, then grasped the handle like a battle staff.

"What you schemin' on doing with that?" Roy asked, bristling.

"What?" Ketch asked with an incredulous tone. "This here oar?"

"Yeah, that oar. You ain't gonna do nothin' with that oar."

"What?" Ketch asked again. "You think I'm gonna reach up there, sweep you off your feet, and wallop you across the forehead with it? We both know that's not gonna happen. Even if you look away I don't have much of a shot."

"That's right," Roy said, raising his 12-gauge into a more commanding pose. "Now drop that oar and come outta that boat."

Ketch softened his stance but said, "I'm not coming out of this boat."

"Get out of that boat or I'll shoot you."

"How can you say I jumped you if you shoot me standing in a rowboat?"

Roy gave that some thought.

Ketch said, "Let me just ask you a couple questions." He figured prolonged conversation might keep him unshot another minute or so.

Roy kept his mouth shut, repartee never being his strong suit.

"One," Ketch asked again, "why are you and Royal stirring up trouble?"

"We ain't been busy enough lately." Roy's answer rang true.

"Why's your pudding-brained cousin always telling you what to do?"

"Royal is dumb as a brickbat, ain't he?"

Ketch hadn't thought of anything else to ask, so he said, "Me and you have always gotten along."

"That ain't even a question. Get out the boat."

"Ain't life hard enough without going out of your way to put hurt on other people?" Ketch asked as he climbed ashore, bringing the oar with him. Roy, taking five quick steps back and aiming his gun in Ketch's face, said, "Get back in the boat."

"Out the boat, in the boat, come on, Roy, we've known each other all our lives, let's act like it."

"You keep comin' up on me, life ain't gonna be too long for you."

"Do unto others, Roy. Let me get on my bike and go."

"I'm gettin' ready to do unto your black ass." Keeping the gun on target, Roy walked over and gave Ketch's bicycle a stomp. He said, "You a grown man. Why you still ride a bike, anyway?"

"Better'n riding in my porky cousin's lap."

Roy smirked. "You hear that?" Somebody was coming. "We'll see who's askin' all the questions when Royal and WW get back here."

He turned his back on Ketch and started waving hello.

* * *

Later, from behind the steering wheel of her car, Dubois Bailey said, "I'm telling you, when I drove up, I was so shocked to see Ketchum whack Roy Elberm over the head with an oar, that the shotgun falling from Roy's hands hardly registered. I was baffled. Felt like the Twilight Zone. Like I should be looking for Rod Serling."

"And then Ketch tied Roy up?" Mary asked.

"With rope from Uncle Nut's boat," said Dubois. "He tossed him in my trunk and put the bicycle in there with him. He threw Roy's shotgun in the back seat, and jumped up here with me. He was scared, but calm."

"Did you think Roy was dead?"

"I was trying to understand, trying to follow what my brother was telling me."

Mary reached from the passenger seat and held Dubois's right hand. Dubois said, "We took Roy to the cove and tied him to Audrey Hepburn. He was hollering some awful vile things, but nobody's going to hear him until they go back there. We tossed Ketch's bike in the weeds on the side of the road so they could see it if they looked hard enough.

"Meaning they'll find Roy, but probably not tonight."

"They'll be looking for Ketch."

"The shotgun?"

"Ketch took it."

"They'll know somebody helped him."

"They'll put you in on it first," said Dubois. "They've already imagined you two in a red-hot love affair. Once they realize he's gone, and then you're gone too, that'll blow all their fuses. They won't consider me until they stumble across Roy or I don't clock in for work in the morning."

"Ketch should have come with you."

"He told me to track you down, grab what we needed, plus his tools and some of his clothes, and to meet him at the packing house right after dark. Then he told me to tell you that if we were ever going to leave, now would be the time," she said, pulling the car to the side of the road.

Dubois turned to Mary and asked one last time. "Are you sure about this?"

"I am," said Mary.

"What about Tooey? Leaving a child behind won't be a paltry thing. This is always going to weigh heavy on you."

Mary was fragile but resolute. "I'm convinced it's what's best. Wesley and I are miserable, and Tooey wants to be with Wesley's parents. Ruth and Moviestar are already raising him. There are days I've been so low... it's not good for a child."

"I just want you to take this last chance to think," Dubois clasped Mary's hands in hers now. "This is the night our lives could change. But you have a baby. I couldn't live with myself if I didn't ask you to reconsider."

"All those times the three of us used to talk about leaving," Mary said, the evening deepening around them. "About where we would go and what we'd do when we lived somewhere we fit in. Somewhere you could be who you're meant to be, somewhere Ketch could rise above being the uppity dock boy, where I wouldn't always be looked at sideways, wouldn't always be called names behind my back."

"I know what they call you."

Mary plowed on. "Remember as we got older, how Ketch started growing more responsible, putting dampers on our fantasies of running away? How we started to grow apart?" She felt like crying for her life not lived.

"Somebody got married."

"Somebody's rabbit died and *then* somebody got married." She laughed but wiped away a tear. "Somebody thought that was what she was supposed to do."

Dubois took a few moments. "Staying," she said, "was a done deal after that. And Ketch felt like with Mom-Mom getting up in age, he should be here to take care of her. I felt the same way."

"And now she's in Baltimore with your Uncle Teat."

"We don't have anything. We'll need money."

"I have almost a thousand dollars."

"Years of penny-pinching?"

"And skimming from the pool hall till." Mary touched Dubois's chin, tilted her face to look her in the eyes. She said, "I've heard there's still a jazz scene in Seattle. Maybe you could find a club to sing in."

"What about Ketch?" Dubois wanted to know. "Is this right for him? He's worked hard to make something of himself."

"And he will again," Mary said. "Given a fresh start someplace, Ketch could have his own business instead of just making Rio Wilmur richer and richer."

"Ketch has never had a real chance to show what he can do."

"He could have a better life than he has here. Looking after you has always been his main concern. He won't have to worry anymore."

"And now that you and Ketch have got your husband and his running buddies all riled up, they'll never let him, or *us*, be."

"I feel like I'm at the top of a Ferris wheel. I see everything. We're in it together. There's no going backwards."

After a while, Mary asked Dubois, "Are we really leaving?"

"I guess we are," said Dubois. She made a comedic carnival-ride face that faded into a gentle smile. "But only because I love you so much."

Mary touched her lips to Dubois's. She couldn't remember the last time they'd dared share a kiss.

Dubois still tasted like sweet tea and Old Bay seasoning.

She tasted like home.

Russell Reece

PRIVATE WATER

A day after I turned sixty my neatly groomed, thirty-two-year-old boss at Consolidated Electronics called me into his office and "downsized" my position. "To protect our *(hugely successful, multi-billion-dollar)* company from fierce competitive forces," he'd said. He'd made a phony grimace. "I know it's tough, George."

I went into the men's room and splashed water on my face. I stared at the reflection in the mirror, the gray hair, the sagging chin, the blemished, wrinkled skin. My job of forty years had just come to an end. I was sixty. Dad had passed at fifty-seven. What's left?

I moped around the house for several weeks, taking naps and watching afternoon television. In the middle of an episode of Dr. Phil my wife Nancy turned off the TV. She shoved my feet off the ottoman and sat down. "Look at me, George," she said. "You better find something to do or you're going to have another big change in your life. I can't deal with this."

"What can I do, Nance?"

"Anything. Learn to play the tuba. Build a fort in the backyard."

I would have once laughed at that but nothing seemed funny anymore.

She grabbed my knee and shook it. "They gave you a good package, honey. You can do whatever you want."

I wanted my job back. I wanted to be young again. I went for a walk.

I'd been content with my job as an inventory specialist, my family and friends. I'd never needed anything else. My only interest outside of work was the Baltimore sports teams. I never got into hobbies. Just the word conjured up visions of a bearded old man with wire-rimmed glasses and tweezers building a model ship on the kitchen table. Tweezers. I shivered at the thought.

I walked past a car with a bumper sticker that read: I'D RATHER BE FISHING. When I was younger and living in Michigan I used to fly-fish. From time to time I still think about those long days on the Pine and the Pere Marquette with my buddy, Jimmy Otto. When we were seniors in high-school we made a plan to fish every major river in the state. We probably got to nine or ten before college and the military took over our lives.

The next morning I dug through the basement and pulled out all my gear. I was cleaning cobwebs off the expensive rosewood net I had once splurged on when Nancy came down the stairs. "I'm going to Michigan for a few days," I said. "I'm going fishing."

She smiled. "Good for you," she said.

* * *

On the river-road west of Baldwin I drove past the turnoff to the trestle three times before I found it. It was still a two-path, winding a few hundred yards through the pine forest. Tall weeds and fiddlehead ferns brushed against the undercarriage as I navigated my car to the turnaround at the edge of the river. Signs were posted along both sides of the lane—Private Property, E.T.A., Inc. I stopped and got out.

It was just as I'd remembered—the fresh clean smell of the springfed stream, the stands of cattails, dark water running through the trench on the far side of the granite railroad trestle. I had daydreamed about this place so many times over the last forty years I wondered if I had blown it out of proportion. But now, I was actually here again, *and it was just as I'd remembered.*

I climbed down the bank, squatted on the spongy apron and ran my fingers through the water. A pair of barn swallows swooped into their nest under the timbers in the bridge. Small minnows grazed in the slow water along the sandbar where, at fourteen, I had beached my first steelhead. I looked downstream, past the bend where I knew there lay a pile of boulders and a deep pool where I had taken hundreds of browns and rainbows. I closed my eyes and mentally checked off all the other good spots for a mile. This moment alone was worth the eight-hundred mile drive from Delaware.

I glanced up as a new white pickup pulled into the turnaround and came to a stop near my car. A tall, lanky guy with curly brown hair, in his late thirties and wearing a khaki shirt and jeans got out, leaving his door open. He reminded me of my ex-boss. I climbed up the bank. A huge black dog riding shotgun stared intently as I approached. It looked like a lab but was twice the normal size. I glanced at the logo on the open door, the image of a trout covered with the initials E.T.A., Inc., encircled by the words, "Executive Trout Anglers Incorporated." Keeping watch on the dog, I said to the guy, "Hey. How's it going?" He was behind my car making a note of my tag on a pocket-sized spiral notepad.

"What are you doing here?" he said as he slipped the notepad into his shirt pocket, also embroidered with the E.T.A. logo. Over the other pocket was his name, Dick. He was a few inches taller than me, solidly built, with an angular, humorless face.

"I used to fish here as a kid. I caught my first steelhead right there under the bridge." I smiled—nothing.

"This is private property. You need to leave."

"When did it turn private? It used to be open to anyone."

"It's not now."

"Are there any public access points nearby?"

He moved closer, as if he were about to grab me. "Look, buddy. If you don't leave I'm going to have you arrested. If you want information, check at the fly-shop."

My adrenalin started to pump and my body tightened. What an asshole. I glanced at the truck. The dog stood with his feet on the driver seat, his head and neck out the door. I got in my car. The guy moved out of the way as I turned around. I stopped next to him, rolled down my window. "Thanks for all your help. Dick."

His face flushed. I waited a moment and then pulled away. In the rearview mirror I watched him get in the truck. He was right on my bumper as I turned onto the highway. The truck lingered in the lane until I was out of sight.

Okay, it's private now, but the guy didn't have to be such a jerk. I had heard that a lot of the property along the stream had been bought up by small groups from Chicago and Detroit and turned into associations where fat-cats could bring clients or friends and fish good water a few times a year.

On the map at the fly-shop I showed the owner all my old spots. "E.T.A. owns that land now," he said. "And be careful, Dick doesn't fool around. The word is he gets a bonus when he has people arrested." I got my three-day license and directions to the remaining public access points. I scouted them all and hiked the edge of the stream. I'm sure there were fish there but I saw nothing like the honey holes I had known in my youth, nothing like the trestle bridge or the rock-pile that I'd been so close to this afternoon. At least I'd be fishing on the famous Pere Marquette again.

But that night, after dinner, and after several beers in a noisy bar, my encounter with Dick began to bug me. What an obnoxious son-of-a-bitch, him and his dog and his new pickup with the fancy logo. Where would *Dick* be without the E.T.A. behind him? He'd be a Nazi nobody just like my fresh-faced ex-boss who probably got a bonus for eliminating my job. The bastards! I was working for Consolidated Electronics and fishing on this river years before either one of them was born.

At that moment I'd had enough. I couldn't do anything about the job, but I was going to fish this river again, all the old spots, and the hell with Dick and the E.T.A.

The next morning I got up at 4:30am and put on my waders in my motel room. After a short drive, I backed the car into the woods on a side-road a quarter-mile from the entrance to the E.T.A. compound.

I hadn't snuck onto private water since I was in my teens, and now the anticipation and nervous adrenalin took me back to that time on the Big Two Heart, in the Upper Peninsula, when Jimmy and I were caught by the landowner and a Barney Fife look-alike with a shotgun who claimed to be a deputy sheriff. He flashed a badge and we were both pretty scared, not so much of the law, but of being alone in the U.P. wilderness. It was the early sixties, anything could have happened and no one would have ever known. They walked us to our car. Barney took down some information from our driver's licenses and let us go. We've had a lot of laughs about it since but at the time we were just thankful to be free and on our way.

I pulled on my vest, slung the net over my shoulder, and fixed the reel to the butt end of my fly-rod. I left the rod in two pieces as it would be easier to maneuver through the thick woods. I locked the car. There was a full moon but it was overcast and pitch-dark under the trees. I jogged across the road and climbed a wire-mesh fence onto the E.T.A property. I would avoid the trestle area, sure that Dick checked it regularly, but there were plenty of other good spots and most would be hidden from the road. Once I got to the stream I would be okay. Getting back to the car could be dicey but I would deal with that when the time came.

I stood by the fence and let my eyes adjust. The woods were still and damp, saturated with the rich scent of pine and cedar. In the distance I heard the faint sound of a truck downshifting to a stop at the light out on M37. As the truck began to accelerate I started toward the water.

The felt soles of my boots were quiet on the pine needle carpet but with every step the waders creaked and the fly-boxes and equipment in my vest pockets rattled. In full gear and rod in hand, I felt like a soldier heading off to battle, the unsuspecting enemy asleep a quarter mile away.

I had gone a few hundred feet when the woods closed in and became a blur of dark columns and shapes of indiscernible composition and distance. I stopped and looked back to reorient myself. *Was that the sound of water off to the left?*

I started that way, probing with my rod like a blind man. I finally dug in my vest pocket for my penlight.

Holding the penlight high above my head, I did a short blast forward and to my right. Then I turned to my left and was stunned to see a cabin and the tailgate of the white E.T.A. truck in the momentary flash. It must be the caretaker's house, and less than fifty feet away. As quietly as I could I moved to the right, flipping on the light every few steps, dodging trees until I was at a safe distance. I finally sat down on a fallen log and rested.

A mist drifted through the canopy. I pulled the rain-hat out of my vest and thought about the day at the Big Two Heart again, how it had been cold and misty when we snuck in before daybreak. It had become one of the legendary adventures of our youth which Jimmy and I relived countless times, especially in the presence of good friends and alcohol. But it was kid stuff, and now just a frivolous counterpoint to forty years of following the rules and loyalty to family and, I shook my head at the thought, the job. I got up and started walking again.

The vegetation grew thicker the closer I got to the stream. I could hear the water. In occasional blasts from my penlight I could see it, but couldn't find a way through and several times got snagged by blackberry vines.

I finally found a spot where the brush opened and the terrain flattened onto a shallow sandbar. I checked my watch; another twenty minutes before daybreak. Without turning on the light I stood at the edge of the water and assembled the rod. I strung the line and after several tries got a new leader out of the package, connected it to the loop and unwound it with no knots.

The sky had turned a shade of gray. The mist hung visibly over the river and leeched into the edge of the woods. A drip came off the brim of my hat. I stood motionless, listening. Aside from the burbling water, the forest seemed unnaturally quiet. And then there was a swishing, like the rush of air through reeds on the beach, and I felt a breath of wind on my neck. I began to turn but a heavy weight pressed down on my head and something pierced the sides of my scalp.

I dropped my rod and flailed with both hands as sharp tines drove deeper into my skin. Then something was moving; flexing, flapping and I fell on my knees as my scalp felt like it was being pulled from the bone. The weight lifted and my hat came off. I grabbed it as a huge owl moved away from me, flapped three, four times and then soared across the river and into the darkness.

"Jeez!" *Did that really happen?* I felt sticky wounds on the side of my scalp. A stream of blood ran down my cheek. *Did he think I was a tree-stump?* With my rain-hat on and standing still in the dark, I guess it would have been an easy mistake. I found some tissues in my vest and dabbed at the wounds.

I started to get up but sensed something hurtling toward me. I ducked just as the owl made a second pass. "Son of a bitch!"

I crouched alongside a tree and peered into the shadowy darkness. Blood filled my sideburn. A short stick lay nearby. I picked it up and held it with both hands as more blood oozed down the back of my neck. I was shaking. I pressed my body against the tree, my knees against my chest. This wasn't what I had planned.

A light rain started. Through the drips of water rolling off the brim of my hat I kept guard as the darkness faded away. Blood continued to ooze. I wondered how many rat or opossum guts those talons had dug into tonight before piercing my scalp. I needed to get to a clinic.

I disassembled my rod and headed back. After a few minutes I could see the fence in the distance and the roof of the caretaker's cabin several hundred yards to my right. I walked quickly in a slight crouch, shielding myself wherever possible behind small trees and bushes. My heart sank into my stomach when the dog began to bark.

I ran. The barking became furious. I had never heard a more terrifying sound. I was fifty feet from the fence when the huge animal crashed through the brush behind me. I turned to face him, backing up, holding the sectioned rod like a rapier. He continued the charge but stopped ten feet away and paced sideways, sniffing the air. He barked again, the sound coming from deep in his stomach, more a belch than a bark. Then he wagged his tail. I couldn't believe it; he was a big teddy-bear. Thank God!

"Good boy," I said. And then over at the cabin the truck engine started. I caught glimpses of the white cab through the bushes as it hurtled down the lane. I turned and in a few seconds was at the fence with the dog trotting happily alongside.

I made it over but my net caught in the wire mesh and as I tried to untangle it the dog jumped at the fence and began to bark. Tires squealed in the vicinity of the lodge entranceway. The net was hopelessly caught and as a vehicle accelerated in this direction I jerked with both hands until the rosewood rim broke into pieces and the net pulled free.

When Dick came around the bend, sped by me and slammed on his brakes I was walking nonchalantly down the road, my rod in one hand, the broken net dangling from the other.

Dick got out of the truck and came toward me, his jaw set, his eyes fixed like he meant business. The dog barked incessantly and leapt against the fence as if it wanted to tear me apart. I stopped, glared at the man and shook the net in his face. "If you even touch me I'll have you in jail before lunch time."

Dick stopped inches away, his fists balled at his side. "I told you to stay off this property."

I glanced around. "Does E.T.A. own this freaking road?"

"What are you doing here?"

"Taking a walk."

"You always dress like that when you go for a walk?"

"Yes, I do." I pushed by him and continued down the road. The dog followed growling and barking, slamming his paws against the wire mesh.

"What happened to your head, old man?" Dick asked.

"Mosquitoes."

"I'm going to be talking to the sheriff about you."

Without turning around I waved.

Dick got in the truck and puttered along ten feet behind me for several minutes until I crossed onto the side-road. He did a wheel-squealing u-turn and sped back to the compound.

As I approached my car I thought of the long drive out here, for nothing; the beautiful river of my youth just across the road, I'll never get to fish. What a foolish idea this was. The Nazis won again.

I popped my trunk, flipped in the bloody hat and started to throw in the net, but stopped. I held it up and turned it from side to side. Several rosewood pieces dangled awkwardly from the nylon fabric. It looked like some kind of aboriginal musical instrument. A few minutes ago I had shaken it in Dick's face. Ridiculous. I was just attacked by an owl. This whole morning had been ridiculous. And all at once it hit me: *I'm sixty years old, straight as an arrow, and I just tried to sneak onto private property to go fishing. I think I've lost my mind!* I began to laugh, and I'm not sure why, but for the first time in over a month the debilitating feeling of oldness and despair suddenly washed away.

I was okay. I was back.

Pat Valdata

SYNESTHESIA

I didn't realize I had walked in front of a car until I smelled onions. Not the sweet fragrance of sautéed onions that caramelize in butter to a rich brown, but the sour odor of overripe onions rotting on a refrigerator shelf.

I turned my head toward the smell, and there was the car, not a foot from my left hip, and the driver, furious from fright, leaning out of the window, mouthing anger at me. I shrugged, shook my head, pointed at my left ear, and continued walking to work.

I was born deaf, but I didn't know I was deaf. No, that isn't accurate; I could see my mother's lips moving, and saw that she and my father had a secret way of communicating with each other. But I thought it was a secret that belonged to grownups, one I would share when I grew up myself. We lived on a farm when I was a small child, and I didn't have any brothers or sisters. But I wasn't lonely. I had the cows for company, and liked to climb up on the old-fashioned milking stool and lean against their brown flanks, feeling their chests bellow in and out. Even as a toddler, I helped my father wash their plump udders and attach the milking machine nozzles to their soft teats. I would walk down the row of cows, patting their heads as they munched hay, and I was very happy.

When I was five, the tractor overturned as my father was hauling a log out of the woods. He was crushed to death, and everything changed. We had to sell the farm, and move to the city, where my mother got a job as a clerk-typist at the Adkins School for the Deaf. No one called it hearing-impaired back then. At school I met other children like me. We were taught to sign, in addition to the usual subjects, and in high school each of us was taught a trade as well. My only natural talent was for milking cows and feeding chickens, so I enrolled in the only remotely bucolic class I could find: landscaping, which at Adkins was little more than learning to re-pot seedlings and arrange cut flowers.

But the work suited me. I enjoyed scooping moist dirt into smooth plastic pots, tamping the humus and perlite around delicate green stems. I liked working with rose geraniums best, and with hyssop, whose licorice leaves perfumed my fingers. Arranging flowers was not so primordially satisfying, but I felt almost like a painter as I coaxed carnations and mums and orchids into rounds and ovals, mixing or matching colors to recreate the golds and greens I remembered from the farm.

The headaches started when I got my first period. The Adkins School didn't go near sex education, and my mother had never attempted to sign a birds and bees lecture. So I was stunned the morning I woke to it, and I ran to my mother in tears, gesturing incoherently, trying to sign the pain in my head and the blood between my legs. She put her hand to her mouth when she understood, and then she kissed me and signed that I shouldn't be afraid. She showed me how to use a napkin, and gave me aspirin for the pain. Then we sat for a long time, while she explained, often having to spell the words letter by letter. And the whole time she signed I smelled freesias.

After graduation I got a job at a florist shop, where they write down the orders, and then show them to me. I don't have to work the cash register because that person also has to answer the telephone; I just work at a table in the back, near the coolers, surrounded by baby's breath and roses and fern fronds, wires and foam blocks and ribbons.

Mrs. Spallucci, who owns the shop, has learned a few basic signs: hello, good bye, thank you. She signed hello when I walked in after my encounter with the car. The smell of sour onions was fading, but I could feel the headache starting at my temples. The doctor says they are migraines, and no one really knows what triggers a migraine, but I know the smells trigger mine. I wanted to get as many orders finished as I could before it got too bad.

I was glad the smell of flowers didn't hurt the way lightning did. Maybe it's thunder that smells, I have no way of knowing, but when I see the flash I always smell burnt toast, and if the storm passes quickly I'm okay, but sometimes, in the summer, there's lightning for hours, and a headache always follows.

I used to get headaches every day, mostly mild ones, until I learned to ignore the smells that hurt, and focus on the kind ones, like the smell that birds make on spring mornings, sweet as honeysuckle.

But when I'm startled by a powerful smell, like the rancid onions on my way to work, then I get a bad headache, and this would be no exception, I could tell. Colored lights danced and shimmered in front of my left eye. I would like the way they looked if they didn't signal the coming of so much pain. I managed to make one arrangement, mostly yellow, for a birthday, and another, bigger arrangement, with lots of red roses, for an anniversary. Then all I could do was hold my head and weep.

Mrs. Spallucci touched me on the shoulder. She reeked of worry, a cloying stuffy scent, like stargazer lilies.

"I am going to call your mother," she mouthed.

Twenty-three, and I still live at home, but what can I do? My mother needs me. Not to cook and clean, although I help as much as I can, but to be there for her. I used to ask her, years after my father died, why she wouldn't see anyone else. But she would only shake her head, and sign to me that she married for life, like a Canada goose, and like the goose she would spend the rest of her life missing her mate.

Sorrow smells like decaying leaves. Sweet and rotten at the same time.

I don't know how much time passed before my mother arrived, and I nearly suffocated from the lilies of her concern. She and Mrs. Spallucci helped me into the car, but instead of driving me home, my mother went to the emergency room. I wanted to shake my head no, no, but that hurt too much. She helped me out of the car and into a wheelchair, then I had to shut my eyes against the fluorescent glare as she, or someone, wheeled me inside.

They brought me into an examining room. While they helped me onto the gurney some angel shut off most of the lights. I couldn't tell if she was a nurse or a doctor—no one wears uniforms anymore that make it easy to tell. A woman in a white coat can be an internist or a lab technician; a man in scrubs may be a nurse or a surgeon. Most of the people who work there wear white pants and brightly colored jackets that are supposed to look cheerful, but they always remind me of the awful day my father was taken away in an ambulance.

I would hate hospitals and doctors even without my father's accident. I'd seen enough of them when I was first enrolled at Adkins. But today I didn't care where I was, as long as the pain went away.

"They want to give you an MRI," my mother signed.

"I don't care," I signed back. The stargazers made my throat close. I opened my eyes a crack to look at my mother.

"Will our insurance cover it?" I signed.

"Don't worry about it. We have to do something—you can't go on like this." She smiled, but the scent grew even stronger.

"I'm sorry," I signed. She picked up my hand and kissed it, and the odor of worry was blown away by cinnamon and cardamom and citrus, surrounding me like a pomander ball.

The MRI room was blinding white and I winced until they put me inside the machine, the cylinder only a little wider than my shoulders. Inside was darker and odorless until an explosion of cayenne that made me gasp. It faded and grew stronger, faded and grew stronger, until my eyes watered. I was screaming by the time they pulled me out. Someone stuck a needle in my arm. The blessed blackness came on quickly after that.

I woke in a darkened room with a pale green curtain all around me. I moved my head slightly to the right and left, and when nothing happened worse than a small twinge I looked around for my mother, but she wasn't there. My hand was on top of a small plastic cylinder with a button at one end. I pressed the button.

In a few minutes the green curtain opened, letting in my mother and a man in a white lab coat and the worry, but only a whiff of that. More powerful was the unmistakable pungency of pine. We'd gone on a vacation once, long ago, to Colorado, and it reminded me of standing on the continental divide, inhaling the boreal fragrance of conifers and cool, clean mountain streams.

"What's so interesting?" I signed.

My mother squeezed my hand and gestured toward the man.

"This is Dr. Belghali."

"I am pleased to meet you," he signed. I raised an eyebrow in surprise and he smiled. "I guess most doctors you meet don't sign."

"You've got that right."

"My sister is deaf. That's what made me interested in diseases of the ear. But what about you? Are you feeling better?"

"Much better, thank you."

"We gave you something so you could sleep, and a triptan injection that should make your headache go away, almost entirely. I can prescribe the same medicine in a nasal spray so you can treat it yourself next time."

"Thank you."

The pine fragrance became suddenly stronger.

"Tell me what you can smell right now."

"I don't understand," I signed. The pine, though, and something acrid—like a wet bonfire—from my startled mother.

He began to mouth words and sign simultaneously. "I'd like to know what you smell when I speak to you."

Suddenly I was not sure I liked the smell of pine. I closed my eyes but the scent of my mother's worry and confusion made me open them again. I reached for her hand and spelled out "it's okay" into her palm.

"It's not about the way you speak," I signed to the doctor. "It's what you feel when you speak to me."

My mother squeezed my hand to get my attention.

"I don't understand," she signed. "What are you two talking about?"

"I smell emotions, sort of. It's more like the feelings carried by the sounds." I spelled the word letter by letter: S-Y-N-E-S-T-H-E-S-I-A.

"Yes," nodded the doctor. "That's what it's called. How do you know?"

"I looked it up, at the school library," I signed. "When I was in high school. It's rare. Most people who have it sense color when they hear sounds. One stimulus, two senses."

"That's correct," signed Dr. Belghali. "But your ability is rarer still. Have you always been able to do it?"

"Since I was thirteen."

My mother pressed my shoulder. "Why didn't you tell me?"

Stargazers, onions, smoke.

"Would you have believed me?"

The onion smell grew stronger as she began to protest. I gave her a look and sat up in the bed. I signed to both of them.

"At first, I tried telling the kids at school, but they laughed at me, and told the teachers on me. The teachers thought I was lying. I was having adjustment problems, they said, telling tall tales to get attention. You had to meet with them, Mom. Remember?"

My mother nodded.

"So I shut up about it. I didn't want to get in any more trouble. Besides, you had enough to worry about. You had a deaf kid to support."

She began to cry.

"It's okay, Mom. It's really okay." In a moment the harsh, smoky smell began to fade.

"See, soft noises and feelings don't give me a headache, and they smell good, like cut grass. But sudden, angry noises—car horns, exhaust backfiring, things like that—they usually startle people, and loud, repetitive noises irritate them. And any time people speak, there are feelings that go along with it."

Dr. Belghali nodded. "Body chemistry changes with one's emotional state, especially strong emotions. A dog can smell fear."

"Woof, woof," I signed. "It smells like ammonia and it gives me a headache. So do anger, and sorrow, and hate. At first, I thought I had a brain tumor. But it's been ten years, and I'm still alive, so I don't think that anymore. Now I think I'm just a freak."

"You're not a freak," signed Dr. Belghali, "and you don't have a brain tumor. But you do have a very unusual condition. The olfactory lobe of your brain—that's the part that interprets smells—is greatly enlarged, and I'm guessing that the nerves from your inner ear are somehow connected to the olfactory lobe instead of the auditory lobe, which is what normally processes hearing."

"What about the emotions?" I asked.

He shrugged. "That I can't explain without further tests. But I suspect it's an artifact, simply the result of your heightened sense of smell."

"What should we do?" asked my mother.

"What can we do?" signed the doctor. "Even if there were some way to identify the neurons and reroute them, I'm afraid the auditory lobe is atrophied, almost nonexistent. There's no way your daughter will ever hear sound as you or I do."

Dead leaves. Mud flats at low tide.

I reached for my mother's hand. She turned toward me, her cheeks wet with tears.

"Mom," I signed, "it's okay. I'm okay the way I am. It's only the headaches that bother me."

"And those we can control with the new generation of medicines," Dr. Belghali said.

"The smells won't go away, will they?" I asked. I didn't care for the smell of ammonia, or rotten onions or burning mulch, but I couldn't imagine how bland life would be without them.

"No chance of that," signed the doctor. "The pain mechanism is distinct from the olfactory. We'll fix the pain, or at least make it bearable, but the other is a normal part of who you are."

Normal. I don't think any doctor had ever used that word to me before.

We left the hospital a few hours later. My mother watched me closely as we walked out the door. I think it was the first time she really noticed the angry sounds of the jackhammers, the car horns, the elevated train. On the city street, I was assaulted by emotions that mimicked knife blades in my head.

We moved away shortly after that, out of the city, to a house in the country, where the birds waft jasmine, and the bleating of spring lambs smells as soothing as a mug of hot cocoa.

We live a couple miles from a small town with a nice little florist shop that I can bike to any day the weather is nice. My headaches are rare, now, and when I get them they aren't nearly so bad thanks to the new prescription. My mother works as a bookkeeper for the local real estate agent, and we spend our evenings together gardening. Our landlord is a dairy farmer, and I like to get up early and help him wash the cow's udders, and while the ladies are milked I walk along the row and pat their heavy black and white heads.

Their lowing smells like lilacs.

NONFICTION

Maisha Britt

THE LIFE JOURNEY OF MARTHA BEA

Martha and Martin were five-year-old twins, living with their mother, Mrs. Sena, in a small South Carolina town in the early 1950s. The twins were in the first grade attending elementary school in Possum Hollow. Miss Dial, their teacher, made it a priority to teach Martha to use her right hand to write instead of her left hand. At the request of Mrs. Sena, the teacher would place a pencil in Martha's right hand and guide her in writing her ABC's and numbers, one to ten. Miss Dial would have the class practice writing their letters and numbers for twenty minutes each school day. When the teacher would return to her desk, Martha would reverse the pencil back to her left hand to continue to practice her writing. By the time she finished the first grade, Martha could write well with both hands. Miss Dial discussed this with Martha's mother, and told her that due to her determination and tenacity, her child would, most likely, do amazing things in her lifetime. At this early age, Martha had learned to master two tasks during the same time. Mrs. Sena knew that both her children were special to her and in many ways.

Mrs. Sena Goes to the Hospital

The twins' grandmother, Miss Sis, lived about one mile from Mrs. Sena's home. One afternoon, Martha and Martin were picked up from their second-grade classroom and taken to their Granny's house. They were told that their mother had to go into the hospital for a few days and they would be staying with her until their mother came home. This news was shocking to the twins because they had never been separated from their mother except while in school. They would go everyplace together. They asked if Granny would take them to see their mother, but were told that the hospital was in another town, and she had no way to take them, as she did not have a car. Miss Sis also told them that children were not allowed to visit in the hospital. As their grandmother was preparing dinner and evening was drawing near, Martha became anxious for her mother. She slipped out the front door and walked along the railroad tracks and up to Washington Heights to reach her home. She began knocking on the door and calling for her mother to open the door, as if she did not believe that she was away in the hospital. She sat on the porch swing and cried as if abandoned. Soon her grandmother showed up with a switch in hand. That was the first time her grandmother had ever chastised her, explaining that anything could have happened to her, and to make sure that she did not do that again. Martha could see that her Granny was worried, not only for her leaving her house, but also for her daughter, Mrs. Sena. After walking back to her house, Granny embraced the twins, praying with them for their mother to be well and to come home soon. And after dinner, all was well and at peace again.

Mrs. Sena Comes Home from the Hospital

Miss Sis and the twins arrived early at Mrs. Sena's on the day she was to come home from the hospital. She was as anxious to see them as they were to see her. There were hugs and kisses and squeals of "Mama, Mama" from the children. What a happy time it was for everyone! Mrs.

Sena had been in the hospital for three days. She showed her mother, Miss Sis, the bandages and dressings covering a surgical area on her left breast. The children realized that whatever had happened to their mother was serious. From that moment on, they did not let her out of their sight. Granny stayed to help her daughter for a few more days, and then returned to her home. Martha would not go outside to play, as her mother had to stay in bed a lot until she would return to her doctor to have sutures removed. When she would go to the bathroom, the twins would stay near the door until she came back out to get in bed. One day, Martha was sitting on the bed waiting for her mother to come out of the bathroom. She thought it was taking her too long this time. She knocked on the door, calling out to her, but her mother did not answer. The door was locked. Martha panicked. She ran out onto the porch screaming, "Help! My Mama! Help me!"

Neighbors nearby went into the house, and someone broke open the bathroom door. Martin had run over to get his grandmother and she hurried back with him. Mrs. Sena had passed out on the bathroom floor, and her bandages were soaked where her sutures had come undone during her fall. By this time, her doctor and an ambulance had arrived, and she was taken back to the hospital. The doctor said that she might not have made it if the children had not been paying close attention to her. He said that the incision had become inflamed, but they would take care of her, and she would be better in a few days.

Mrs. Sena returned to her home after two more days in the hospital, feeling better, but was still on bedrest for another two weeks. Her mother stayed with her to make sure that she had her meals and medications on time every day, and to take care of the children.

Martha Makes Up a Song for Her Mother

Mrs. Sena's bedroom was next to the living room, which held an upright piano on the opposite wall. Her bed was on the opposite bedroom wall. Martha would climb up on the piano bench and make up music to entertain her mother. As her mother lay in bed recuperating,

Martha asked her, "Mama, what are the words on the mottos up on the wall?"

Her mother answered her, and Martha began to sing the words in a song to her as she played the piano: "Christ is the Head of this House. Jesus Never Fails. The Lord is My Shepherd, I Shall Not Want. Christ is the Head of this House!"

Martha played the piano and sang the song to her mother, repeatedly. When she finished and turned around, Mrs. Sena had gotten out of bed and was sitting in a chair in the living room, adoring her little girl as she sang her new song to her.

She said to Martha, "Your song has helped me to heal and get well!" She added, "I thank the Lord for you and your love." Mrs. Sena kissed Martha on her cheek and said, "Now, let's go into the kitchen and make some dinner!"

Martin was outside playing in the yard with his cousins until dinner was ready.

Mrs. Sena Goes to Work

Mrs. Sena worked as a caretaker for Mrs. McDaniel, whose health was failing. The McDaniel's owned a big tire company in town. On weekdays, she would take the five-year-old twins to work with her. This was agreeable with Mr. and Mrs. McDaniel, since she did not want to have her mother, Miss Sis, spend time watching them, because she had her own dressmaking and quilting business to operate. Miss Sis made dresses, blouses, skirts, and baby clothes for families. She would measure each customer and make patterns to cut out the materials. She made shirts, pants, and suits for men customers. She would knit and crochet baby clothes and blankets for newborns at their family's request. Miss Sis made quilts for her children, and for each newborn grandchild, and would take orders from many people in town and surrounding areas.

During her first week of work at the McDaniels, Mrs. Sena did leave the twins with her mother, but they continued to ask for her. They missed her and were always asking, "When is Mama coming to get us?"

They became more anxious for her day by day. On the third day, she took them for a walk and showed them where their mother was working. They returned to Granny's house and were happy, although they did not actually see her. On the next day, the twins went out to play in their grandmother's yard, and after a little while, she did not hear their voices anymore. She called out to them, but they did not answer. Miss Sis walked through the neighborhood, searching, but did not see them. She walked to her daughter's workplace and saw them sitting on the top step of the red brick porch, at the McDaniel's house.

She asked them, "Why did you leave the yard without asking me? You are too young to be walking all the way over here without a grownup." She continued to fuss at them. "What if somebody had snatched you and took you off somewhere, and your mama could never see you again? Is that what you want?"

They answered in unison, "No ma'am, Granny."

Just then, Mrs. Sena came to the front door and said, "I thought I heard voices out here. What happened, why are you here?"

Her mother told her what the twins had done. Mrs. Sena went back into the house and spoke with Mrs. McDaniel, telling her that she might not be able to continue working for her, because the twins had left their grandmother's and had come looking for her and were sitting on her steps waiting for her to come out.

Mrs. McDaniel said, "You need to get a switch and whip them both, so they won't try that again." She went on to say, "It's in the Bible, 'If you spare the rod, you spoil the child'."

Mrs. Sena did not argue with her about her children, but she would not whip her children for missing her and loving her so much.

Mr. McDaniel had closed his store and came home to relieve Mrs. Sena for the day. He spoke to Miss Sis and the twins and went into the house. His wife told him why Mrs. Sena's family were out on the porch. He told Mrs. Sena that he really needed her help, and that she was the only caretaker that Mrs. McDaniel was comfortable with, and asked if they could work something out. They talked it out and he asked Miss Sis and the children to come inside. Mr. McDaniel asked the twins if they wanted a job. They looked at him and then looked at their mother with questions in their eyes.

He said, "You can come to work with your mama, but you will have work to do part of the time when you are here." He went on to say, "I will pay you each thirty-five-cents a week to rake the leaves and put them in bags. You can sweep the front and back porches and your mama can find some other light work for you to do." He added, "This can justify you coming to work with your mama, and you will make money for your piggy bank. How does that sound to you? Can we count on you to come to work with your mama until it's time for you to go to school?"

In unison they both said, "Oh, yes sir!"

Mrs. McDaniel added, "I will give you loose-leaf paper to draw and write your letters and numbers."

The twins said excitedly, "Thank you, ma'am!"

On any day, you could drive down South Harper and see the twins happily raking the McDaniels' leaves. Happy because they could be near their mama at work, every day!

Martha's Scare at The Fourth of July Parade

Things were going well for Mrs. Sena and the twins at the McDaniels. Martha and Martin were doing well, and their employers liked them a lot. It was getting close to the Fourth of July Day Parade, which the town businesses and county government sponsored. Mr. McDaniel asked Mrs. Sena if she wanted to have the twins participate in the parade, and to think about what she would want them to do. He said that his business, the tire company, would sponsor them. She talked to the twins, and Martha said she wanted to be a majorette because Mrs. Sena had just bought her a red, white, and blue baton with silver sparkles on it. She loved to twirl it in her front yard. Mrs. Sena would need to order the uniform, hat, and white majorette boots. Martin told his mother that he did not want to march in the parade, that he just wanted to stay with her. Mr. McDaniel gave Mrs. Sena all the directions and told her the time to have Martha at the starting location.

When they arrived at the starting location, on July Fourth, the town square was already filled with spectators. The parade would be quite colorful. When it was time to line up, Martha was led to her position by the Grand Marshal. Once they started, her mother and brother moved along the sides, keeping up with her position. Martha had practiced marching and baton twirling and was looking like a cute little princess majorette. The parade was moving right along, when suddenly there was a very loud pop, which sounded like a big gun. It was a scary sound that was unexpected to Martha. She took off running as fast as she possibly could from the parade in the direction of her home. She did not look back and she did not slow down one little bit. Mrs. Sena and Martin were running after her and calling her name, but she did not hear them or look back to see if they were coming after her. Martha was traumatized and escaping from something and she did not know what it was. She was in shock.

When her mother and brother did catch up to her, Mrs. Sena told her that it was just an old car backfiring.

"What is backfiring?" she asked.

Her mother explained what it was and said that it was planned to happen that way. She tried to convince Martha to return to the parade and festivities, but she refused.

"Never again!" she said. "No more parades!" She had never heard a gunshot before, but it was the closeness of the loud pop that had frightened her. The old car was just six feet behind Martha's position.

Martha Struck by Lightning

Mrs. Sena had opened a variety store about 100 feet from their house in their small hometown. She wanted to be with her twins and would take them to the store with her each day. One late morning a storm was coming up. The sky had turned very dark, but there was no rain or thunder yet. Mrs. Sena collected the denominations of cash from the register and placed them into the metal cash box and locked it. She and the twins came out of the store to go to their home, and as Mrs. Sena turned to put the jumbo padlock on the door, she handed the cash box to Martha and told her to go on to the house. Martin stood by her side as she locked the door. Just as Martha turned to walk towards the house, a very loud lightning bolt was heard. No thunder, no rain. It struck the metal cash box in Martha's left hand and traveled up her arm. She was knocked about fifty feet onto the back porch of the house across the street from their house. The locked cash box was knocked open and cash was strewn all over the neighborhood, into front and back yards. Martha did not remember anything except hearing the loud lightning strike. She was in a daze for several days and her hair was electrified and static. For a few days, she could not hear on the left side, but then began to complain of pain in her left ear. Mrs. Sena took her to see Dr. Wade. He told her mother that her left eardrum had burst during the lightning strike. He said that it would never heal, but he could see Martha once a week until the pain went away. Dr. Wade put a warm liquid in Martha's ear, and gave Mrs. Sena an appointment time for the next week. Martha was taken to see the doctor for several weeks for her ear problem. Mrs. Sena could not take her one week and she asked her mother, Miss Sis, if she would take Martha to see Dr. Wade for her ear treatment and she did. When the treatment was finished, Miss Sis asked Dr. Wade, "What is that you are putting in her ear."

Dr. Wade said, "It's warm Sweet Oil."

Martha's grandmother said, "Oh, we can do that."

That was Martha's last visit to Dr. Wade for her busted eardrum. Her granny bought Sweet Oil and a dropper on her way home, and she and Mrs. Sena warmed the oil and used a dropper to put it in Martha's ear whenever she had pain. They could not control the static electricity in Martha since the lightning strike, and when they would come near to comb and brush her hair, the braids would rise and waver towards them. This and vertigo would be something that she would have to learn how to overcome as she would adjust to life while maturing.

Martha's First Disappointment

Martha and Martin moved up to the second grade in Mrs. Bea Sullivan's class in Possum Hollow. Mrs. Sullivan was also a neighbor, as many of the other school teachers were in their hometown. This was the first year since starting school that Martha was excited about the Annual May Day School Festival. It was always celebrated the first weekend in May, with many participants. Mrs. Sullivan's class was chosen to be Forget-Me-Not flowers. She was also a seamstress in town and agreed to make the Forget-Me-Not dresses that the girls would wear for their performance. The parents had to purchase light blue chiffon material, thread, hem binding, and a white crinoline slip so the dress could stand out like the petals of the Forget-Me-Not flower. After making the dresses, Mrs. Bea would take each girl's dress to her home for the final fitting before May Day.

Martha stood and looked in the mirror after putting on the blue dress. It was the most beautiful dress she had ever seen. She told Mrs. Bea that she felt like a little princess in blue. She was so excited and could hardly wait to get to school on May Day to wear her blue dress and perform. The festival performances would begin after lunch, in the afternoon. The first-grade classes performed, and then it was time for the second graders to perform. Mrs. Sena had brought Martha's dress, white patent leather shoes, and white socks to school and had helped her to change into them when it was their turn. It had been a clear and bright sunny morning until the Forget-Me-Nots were dressed and ready to go out onto the school yard to take their places. They were to sing their song, curtsy, and do their little dance. The song began as, "We're little tots, forget-me-not, we come all dressed in blue… " It had begun to drizzle as the second-grade classes were lining up to do what they had practiced for the two weeks leading up to the May Day festive event. The rain really began to pour down and the sky turned dark. The teachers and parents quickly gathered the children and hurried them back into the school. Once back in the classroom, Martha asked her mother if they were going to wait for the rain to stop so they could sing their song.

Mrs. Sena said, "No, we are going home now. It is too wet, and the activities are rained out."

Martha asked, "Can we have it tomorrow, or another day?"

Mrs. Sena explained that the other parents, teachers, and students were all leaving school because of the bad weather, as she drove the twins home in her vintage Model-T Ford. Martha could not accept the fact that she could not wear her little blue princess dress, the prettiest dress that she had ever seen in her life. For days, Mrs. Sena tried to help Martha out of her dark blue mood, yet nothing was working, until the twins heard some small sounds coming from underneath the store building in their front yard.

Hero: Martha's Angel Dog

The twins were coming out of the house on their way to the Model-T Ford, when they heard sounds coming from underneath the store building. Mrs. Sena came out of the house and said that it sounded like a newborn puppy. By this time, Martha and Martin had squirmed their way half way under to the middle of the store on the ground to where the puppy was. Together, they took turns inching the puppy from underneath the building out into the light. The little puppy had never been in the light before and was squinting and trying to shield his eyes. He was so little and fragile that he could not even stand up on his own four little legs. Mrs. Sena asked if they saw any other puppies, and they said, "No ma'am, just this one."

Where did he come from? How long had he been under Mrs. Sena's store? Who put him there? Why did someone put him there? How did he get all the way under into the middle of the building? He was only a tiny, little black puppy, unable to get himself from under the building, but he was making the little whimpering sounds just at the right time.

Mrs. Sena went back into the house to get a cardboard box and towel to put the puppy in to ride to school with the twins. Before they could leave for school, Mrs. Sena marched them back into the house to wash up and change their clothes. The twins had both squirmed their way under the building to get the puppy and bring it out. After checking, Mrs. Sena told them that it was a boy puppy. They wanted to know if they could keep him, and their mother said, "Yes, it must be your puppy to be all the way under the store and being a new born."

There was a fence surrounding their property, a gate at the beginning of the front walk, and a double gate at the driveway. No matter, there was no way the tiny puppy could get to where he was found on his own. The building was not very high from the ground, and the six-year-olds had had to squirm and slide on the dirt to get to him.

Mrs. Sena asked neighbors and others in the town if their dogs had delivered a litter, but the answers were "No." They were always looking, but never saw any dogs that looked like the puppy. Mrs. Sena asked the twins what they wanted to name their new puppy.

Martha said, "Let's call him Hero, like the dog in the story book that saved the little girl from drowning in the lake."

Their mother would always buy books and read stories to them daily. Hero turned out to be the perfect name for their new puppy, for as he grew, he was always there for Martha in her times of perils and need. He became her best friend, and then her angel pet, because of all that he was, all that he did, and because the mystery of his beginning was never solved.

Charles Brent Cole

BOUNDARIES

When I took a philosophy course on crisis and commitment, I learned that life, as I picture it, contains boundaries I form to make myself feel safe. They're formed from my beliefs, experiences, faith and knowledge. I feel confident that if I do not step outside of these boundaries, I will be okay.

But then there's the world. It doesn't seem to care much about where I place those boundaries. Occasionally, it's going to reach into its bag of tricks and send me something that shatters my boundaries ferociously and instantly. The big ego, known as me, will deflate like a pricked balloon. I'll be left defenseless, naked and scared. It will bring me to my knees, and for a little while, I will see the nothingness from which god made me.

So it was on a sunny day in a northern industrial city, far from home. On that day, I drove a tractor-trailer to make a delivery of frozen dinners to a commercial-freezer warehouse. One more stop and I could reload for another delivery to Landover, Maryland, at a supermarket distribution center. It's a good feeling when the truck is unloaded. It means you've made your money and now, you're ready to make some more.

Trucks make a lot of noise. A truck driver learns to hear the pace of the engine, the rattling of the reefer unit, a squeak in a spring, the hiss of the air tanks. They become part of the mindset, the flow of the day, along with the traffic lights and the street and highway signs. But let a foreign sound break that flow, and the boundary that tells a truck driver that everything is okay flashes red. It may be nothing, but it must be checked out.

Drivers are tense when they pull over to explore one of these warnings. Did the metal reefer door fall off? Will I be stuck here for two days getting repairs? My appointment for offload was in ten minutes; will I still make it on time or lose my spot and have to wait three more hours, and then miss my return load? I thought of all this, as I swung out of the cab onto the first step, grabbed the handrail for support, and lowered myself carefully to the street.

I wonder now, when do the boundaries begin to shatter? For those on the Titanic, was it when the ship hit the iceberg, or when it finally sank? For Oedipus, was it when he murdered his father, or when he vowed to find his killer? For me, was it when I first heard the odd noise, or when I saw the bicycle, half of which was under my tractor's tandem axles?

There was a moment, when my boundaries were melting, that time stopped; it was as if the trick had taken hold of my head and was forcing me to watch a still of the transition. This is your new world, it said; now go! When time moved again, the world of just a few seconds ago was gone forever.

I stood there, naked and exposed, with no boundaries to protect me. I still see her, the ten-year-old girl, lying there, twisted, mangled, crushed. My fellow creatures said I looked before I made the turn, and that she did this dangerous thing all the time, dodging the trucks. And her mother, who walked up and asked, "Is that my daughter?" But no one knew, because whoever she was, she wasn't anymore.

I remember my philosophy instructor saying,"Humpty Dumpty has fallen off the wall and broken into many pieces. What you do with the pieces, outside your previous boundary—a frightening, foreign place where you have never found yourself before—is what this class will explore."

I ran across the street and into a diner to call the police. But when my trembling hands couldn't push the "911" buttons, a man whose face I can't remember made the call for me.

I ran back to my truck. The crowd began to grow; from several, to numbers that didn't matter anymore. I grabbed the sheet from my sleeper berth and covered her as best I could. I pleaded with them to move away. But still, they came.

"What happened, man?" and "God Damn!" and "Are you okay?" were tossed over the wall by those standing outside of my new world. But I was a sentry, ignoring them, protecting her. I told them what I was trained to tell them, that I am not allowed to make any statements until the police come.

Then the cameras came; Action News some-number, with the pretty young woman bursting through the crowd, microphone in hand, "Can you tell us what happened here?" and "How do you feel right now?" As if there could be words with which to tell her.

The policeman arrived. Get back, he ordered the crowd. As they moved away, I felt an unexpected sense of relief. It came from the sound of the policeman's voice—not from over the wall like the other voices, but talking directly to me. For the first time, I was not alone. The adrenaline powered robot gave way to the broken man; the sentry could stand down.

I looked at the policeman, another person whose face I can't remember now, then down at the sheet. For the first time, I burst into tears. Up to then, the child in me clung to the hope that somehow this wasn't real. But it was, and those tears were watering the seeds of acceptance. He waited patiently, until I was able to speak again.

I told him what had happened. We finished the paperwork and stood waiting for the coroner, who was busy that day and was delayed. He arrived. I see him, even now, as he stepped out of his car, wiping his brow with a handkerchief, a man busy at work; someone who, at least on this day, was enjoying his job.

"Damn," he said, looking towards the sheet. "It's a bad day for bicycles. This is my second one today."

As he walked towards the sheet, a cold, frightening feeling filled me. I realized I was about to see it all again, except this time, I had all my senses. The hopeful child in me could not be found. When he pulled back the sheet, the seeds of acceptance began to sprout, and I understood why Oedipus had gouged out his eyes.

I remember only one other thing from the scene of the accident: the words "Okay driver, you can go now." I must have moved the truck to free the bicycle; I must have seen them take her away; but even now, I don't remember it. And how did I drive to the warehouse to make my delivery? But I did. I had to. There was no one else to do it.

There would be no return load that day. I went to a truck stop and parked somewhere among the other dozens of trucks, one among many. I don't remember doing that either; I just remember being there. Could anyone have guessed my empty truck weighed so much, or that I sat behind the wheel sobbing, hoping to lighten it?

Many things happened that day. The ones I remember will be with me for the rest of my life; images like the pretty lady from Action News some-number, who came on the television to give her breaking news while I was sitting in the drivers lounge; or the last thing I remember about that day, the two young ladies who approached me outside the truck stop, neither more than sixteen, who sat down on the bench next to me.

"Would you like a date Mister?" one of them asked. But when tears, instead of words, came as their answer, they withdrew.

I don't remember leaving the bench to go to the truck, and I don't remember sleeping in the truck; I don't remember what cargo I loaded the next day, or where I took it. But I do remember that it was two days after the accident before I could finally walk through my own front door.

"It looks like the king's men have left Humpty and gone home," the professor had said. "Humpty has returned to the land he knows. But will he ever be home again?"

I didn't know. But I felt sure the journey would be on a path I had not yet traveled, and that distances would be measured in years instead of miles. How could I ever make sense of life again? What about her family—her father, her mother, maybe brothers and sisters? Many boundaries lay shattered, and I was fate's instrument who had wrought the destruction. It would, indeed, be a long way home.

Her mother hadn't stayed long at the scene. She came when I was the sentry, and I only saw and heard her briefly. It seems to me she had said she recognized the bicycle. As best I can remember, she said nothing else, and, with a look of disbelief, turned and walked away. I never saw her again.

Had I heard someone say that her father was a truck driver, and that she had a brother? Was there a picture of her on the television during the news broadcast? I don't remember ever seeing a picture of her.

On the way home, I began to think about what this death would do to her family. I pulled off the highway and, from the depths of my insides, cried as if it had happened all over again. But I wasn't mourning for her; I was mourning for her family. I saw parents who had lost a child; I saw siblings too young to understand what had happened, and chaos that knew no end for all of them.

I had become her brother, just two years older than she. I saw her taken away from him, and her mother humbled to the point that it was all she could do to cling to Jesus. I saw her father, an alcoholic, falling head first into his addiction. I felt the guilt of being the oldest child and not having been the one taken. I saw that first Christmas when she wasn't there, but still had presents under the tree; and her first birthday after she was gone. I saw her father drunk and her mother crying.

When two worlds with no boundaries merge within you, you will hope there is a god. At the very least, you will call his name. I don't mean that in an affectionate way. I mean that in a way where you really do think you are looking into the abyss, and he's your last hope; when everything you think you ever knew means nothing, and your next thought will disconnect you from your sanity. And if much more is revealed, you will be glad of it.

I wasn't crying for her brother or her family; this time, I was crying for me. I was her brother. That family was mine! And memories of chaos and a world gone mad filled my being. I realized I was both now; the brother and fate's instrument. And she was my 12-year-old sister who had died of leukemia when I was 14.

For the first time in my life, I realized I was already on a path created by a world with shattered boundaries. The journey was 16 years long. And now, as fate's instrument, I had started another family on theirs. I learned that day that reality sets no limits on the number of times your boundaries may shatter, or the number of people that shattering might take down with it.

I questioned God about that, but got no answer. Both Gods: the one my mother told me worked in mysterious ways and who, one day, would fix everything; and the one my father told me about who was a no-good son-of-a-bitch for killing my sister. I know no more today than I did then, why things like this have to happen. But they do, and they never stop.

I don't remember all of the details of the five philosophy courses I took, but I can remember the professor's simple rule: as long as it makes logical sense, you can learn more; but, the closer to absolute truth you get, the more difficult it will be to approach it with logic. It will be too magnificent for a mortal mind to comprehend. In the end, if you are wise, you will not lose your way in these places and decide it isn't truth just because you can't understand it.

I spent a lot of time with questions such as "Why me?" and, "If there is a God, why does he let things like these untimely deaths happen to children?" I know now these are fool's questions. No such answers come to us in this life. For those questions, there is only acceptance, if peace is to be found. It took me a long time to understand that.

I will never know if I looked before I made that turn. I expect that has always been the first and foremost question in my mind. But what would I learn to find that I did or did not look before I made that turn—that it was my fault, or that it was not? Would it have stopped me from drifting in and out of my marriages, or drifting in and out of my addictions? Would I have changed my mind and had a family of my own? It has taken getting old to stop asking questions like that.

When I need to center myself, I go to a cemetery in the small rural community where I grew up. Many years ago as a teenager—and then as a young man—I got drunk and went there to cry on my sister's grave. As time passed, her grave was joined by those of my mother, my father, and then, in 2003, another sister.

Now, when I go there, I see the natural order of things coming into being. Six generations of my family are there.

Somehow, my sister's grave complements that picture as perfectly as the sun complements the sky. My anger and resentment have long since lost the strength to exist there. Not because I have forgotten those wretched memories of her death, which haunted me for all those years, but because I have accepted it to be as much a part of life as was her living. All I did, finally, after struggling for a long time, was lay down the questions with no answers, answer those I could, and yield my will to both. Acceptance finally blossomed. But no such acceptance came to me about the accident.

I began to look for the differences. I was not responsible for my sister's death, but, concerning the accident, no such grace will ever be mine. I will always be fate's instrument, at fault or not. Acceptance will have to include that. And I have long since surrendered to those questions which have no answers. What was I missing? I came to this point in my story and could go no further. Then, some months later, I thought of another lesson from my philosophy classes.

It is just as important to answer the questions that have answers as it is to yield to those that do not. Either, left unfinished, blocks the door to acceptance and creates a boundary between myself and it.

Boundaries are the illusions I create when I am afraid to face what I imagine lies behind them. Our lives shouldn't be spent building and repairing boundaries; they should be spent tearing them down!

I finally understood.

I have always been afraid to go anywhere near her, and have never felt it appropriate to contact anyone in her family. I saw no possible good that could come of doing so and imagined plenty of harm for myself. I have imagined her in every young girl's face I see. But imaginings are not truth, and they will never bring acceptance. They bring only unanswered questions—and boundaries.

When I realize I must take down a boundary, imagined or not, I become anxious. My mouth goes dry. I become tense. I doubt myself. I remember Oedipus and what his vow to know the truth brought him. I think about how outside of my imagined boundary lie all the things I fear the most—and none of them play by any rules I can understand.

With the lump still in my throat, I called a private investigator who, in less than two weeks, found the information I needed to begin taking down the boundary. As the gentle lady from the agency began to read, my heart pounded: "Suddenly, in. . ., July 30, 1979, beloved daughter of. . .; dear sister of. . .; granddaughter of. . .; also survived by aunts, uncles and cousins. . .; a student at school. ..."

When she finished, I could not speak. She waited for me to recover, and then she told me they had information about her gravestone. First, she read the dates inscribed on the stone. She had died three days before her eleventh birthday. The kind lady paused a moment, and then gently spoke her nickname. That sound brought to life her stolen childhood innocence and humbled me as nothing had done before. For the first time ever, I allowed the child in me to cry for his. At that moment the walls of my imaginary boundary crumbled, and the light of truth began to shine.

I thanked her for the information. For a while I remained in my chair, taking it all in. I knew I had done the right thing, but I knew I wasn't finished. The next day, I began almost the same journey I had made 33 years ago. I drove until evening, and got a room about an hour from the cemetery. That next morning, each minute I drove toward the cemetery filled me with anxiety. But I knew I would not turn back.

I don't consider myself a religious man, but I know when I am walking on holy ground. As I walked the cemetery searching for her grave, I was afraid—afraid of scaring her because of who I was; afraid someone from her family would see me; afraid that even this, the last thing that would ever be revealed to me about the accident, might not be enough for me to set her spirit free and gain at least the start of acceptance.

As I approached her gravestone, I trembled. I read those same words the kind lady on the phone had spoken to me. But nothing could have prepared me for the picture of her mounted on the gravestone. I fell to my knees, and for a long time I knelt there and cried. More than once, I called out God's name. As the tears fell, and I adjusted to my new reality, I knew those were the tears I had wanted to cry for so long, but had not known how. As I looked at her picture, I knew I had reached the point where no more answers would ever be mine. She was a beautiful child.

So many thoughts went through my mind that afternoon, as I sat there with her. By the end of the day, I believe our spirits connected. I felt forgiven; there was no longer a boundary between her and me. My fear had melted. I felt her there with me, as if it was a day long overdue for both of us. I told her about my sister, and I even imagined the two of them playing together in some sort of children's heaven. There is little more I can do now, for her or for me. Perhaps, when I'm where she and my sister are now, all will be one as is hoped for in religion and in philosophy.

There were no obvious signs of anyone regularly visiting her grave. Perhaps most of her family have died or moved away after all these years. But, for as long as I live, she will never be forgotten. Each year, on July 30th, the day of the accident, and to last through August 2nd, her birthday, I have flowers placed on her grave by a local florist. So far, the florist has told me, there have been no other flowers there when they have taken mine.

Before I left the cemetery, I wrote a short note, placed it in a plastic wrapper, and left it beneath the child-angel ornament sitting in front of her gravestone. Fate will have to decide whether anyone finds it. But I knew if I didn't leave it, her family would have no chance of ever knowing how I have felt for all these years, and how sorry I am for what happened. Maybe they too have questions. I'm sure they have imagined me many times.

Her cemetery is like my family's cemetery—no boundaries can be found in either. I will never go to my family's cemetery again that I do not think of her, and the afternoon I spent with her. When I go, I will not seek answers to questions that have none. Instead, I will surrender my will to that magnificent thing called truth, whose brilliance blinds us all but whose light we must have if our seeds of acceptance are to grow.

Walter F. Curran

A LONG WEEKEND

Pain made me see the light.

When you're a thirteen-year-old punk, hanging around with nineteen and twenty-year-old other punks, you don't realize you're the go-fer and butt of most jokes. You only know you're one of the "guys." It's amazing how much "stupid" you can demonstrate when your sole focus is to impress other people. "Stupid" becomes exponential when the people you're trying to impress are themselves stupid.

Early Friday night, late March 1957. Warm for this time of year, around 65 degrees. Sitting on the top tier of the corroded, wooden slat seats of "M" Street park, shuffling our feet on the filthy concrete, staring at nothing in particular, five of us sat, shot the breeze and waited for Bobby to arrive.

I, William, thirteen, 5'10" tall, 240 lbs. of flab, crew cut blond, am the baby of the group, albeit the biggest, physically.

Billy and Dizzy, brothers, eighteen and nineteen respectively, resemble each other enough to be twins. Each 5'7" and weighing 140 lbs. top, they have a collective IQ of about 70 and proved it by fighting anyone at the drop of a hat. Whatever one started the other joined in and usually finished.

Eddie, twenty, 5'8", 170 lbs., flaming red hair that spiked in all directions, uncontrollable, like his temper. Got in a lot of fights and lost most of them, even lost to me because I got him on the ground and lay on him until he calmed down. Everyone laughed at that, even Eddie after he cooled off.

Chico, twenty, 5'6" 150 lbs., curly black hair, the only non-Irish in the bunch. He was Italian and got his nickname because no one could pronounce his real name, Francescoandreas. Chico was peaceful unless he was drunk, which was every weekend.

At 7:00 pm, Bobby arrived. Bobby was our leader. Mr. Cool. 6'0", 180 lbs., long, brown, slicked back hair combed in a DA in back and an Elvis wave in front. Bobby was nineteen and a natural leader who presumed he was always right. Since his followers were dumb, he was always right, at least in their eyes.

"Hey guys, it's beer time." Was his greeting.

Nods and grunts of acquiescence affirmed his decision. Everyone reached into their pocket, took out two bucks and handed it to Bobby.

Legal drinking age was twenty-one, and no one had a fake ID. Since George, the owner of the local package store, the "packy," knew everyone, a fake ID wouldn't matter. George knew I didn't drink and knew I never had any money, so it was my job to buy the beer. When I came in and handed him ten dollars for ten quarts of Narragansett, Giant Imperial Quarts, saying it was for my dad and brothers, he never even blinked. Walking out of the store lugging the twenty-five pounds of beer, I turned right down "M" Street and the guys were there, waiting in the alley halfway down on the right.

Most Friday nights, if it wasn't raining or snowing, we'd meander down to the beach and sit on the sand. They'd drink, become belligerent, while I mostly sat in silence, absorbing the atmosphere, feeling cool to be one of the guys. This night was different. Bobby decided he wanted to go for a ride. Bobby had a license, but no car. No one else even had a license and, though they wouldn't admit it, didn't know how to drive. City kids. Who needs a car when everyone takes the bus, street car and subway?

I knew how to drive, having learned on a 1945 Willy's jeep on camping trips with the boy scouts. We had rolled that jeep at least fifty times with only minor injuries to us and repairable injuries to the jeep. I also knew how to hot-wire a car. Even Bobby didn't know how to do that, but he knew I did.

"William," Bobby said. "We need wheels. Go get some and meet us here. We're going for a joyride."

This was met with instant approval from everyone, except me. This was a line I hadn't crossed before, stealing a car. Shop-lifting cigarettes and sodas, potato chips and candy bars from the First National Store for the group in the past, no big deal. Now, it was big time.

"C'mon Bobby, why can't we just sit and relax," I said, hoping to duck on this one.

"William," he responded, "You want to be one of the guys, or don't you? We let you hang with us, stick up for you in fights." A lie because they never interceded in one of my fights, even when I was getting my ass kicked. After a pause, Bobby continued, "Well, William? You gonna be one of the guys or you gonna wimp out."

Caving in, I stood and said, "I'll be back," and walked away followed by a chorus of half-assed support.

I needed a wire coat-hanger so I went home and took one out of my Ma's closet then went back to "M" Street looking for an open car window, nervous, knowing it was stupid, but too pushed by my desire to be "included" to back down. Two blocks up the street, I found a 1955 Chevy Bel Air Nomad, a station wagon. Baby blue, two-door, with the flop down tailgate, it had what was necessary, an open fly window.

Twisting the wire to make a loop to slip over the knob of the door lock, I reached through the fly window and popped the lock. Sweating, nerves, not temperature, I opened the door, slid in, closed the door quietly and reached under the dash and pulled the wire array down. Using my switchblade, I cut the harness strap, which loosened the wires, so I could get at them. Doing it by feel, I stripped and coupled the positive and negative "on" wires, then found and stripped the starter wires. Peeking up over the top of the seat to make sure no one was watching, I ducked down, pushed the gas pedal once with my hand to prime the carburetor, touched the wires together to turn the starter motor, and the car started up.

I popped into the driver seat, threw the car in drive, cut the wheel hard right and hit the gas and almost hit an oil delivery truck, sensing it and slamming on the brakes at the last second. The guy gave me a dirty look but kept going and I followed him to 4th street then took a right on 4th to "N" street and rode back to the beach.

Pulling up across from the guys on Marine Road, I beeped the horn. Bobby sauntered over, followed by the pack. Nodding his head, Bobby said, "Nice wheels William."

The Nomad was baby blue with a white roof and white wall tires. Rear fin fenders stuck out like hand rails on either side of the drop-down tailgate. The tailgate had seven vertical chrome bars running from the hinge edge up to the window. Inside were the same colors with the dashboard and doors baby blue and a wide gash of white in the middle of the doors. The bench seat was baby blue where your butt hit it and white at the front edge.

Turning to the guys, Bobby spread his arms and asked, "So, where we going?" then laughed. "Get in," and he opened the passenger side door for them and they piled in, with Chico getting relegated to the back area after arguing with Eddie and losing the finger flip. Bobby took the shotgun seat in front.

Heading down Marine Road towards Dorchester, we went through Andrew Square then turned back and cruised the length of Broadway, not speeding and looking out for cops. The radio was tuned to Arnie "woo-woo" Ginsberg on WBOS 1600 AM as he blasted out the Top 40 hits. Whenever an Elvis song came on everyone in the car joined in. Elvis had five songs on the Top 40 list. The Everly brothers had two songs, "Bye Bye Love" and "Wake Up Little Susie," and we sang along to them. Other than when we passed station #6, there were no cops in sight. We ended up at Castle Island, parked in front of the hot dog shop, closed for the season.

One of Woo-Woo's sponsors was Adventure Car Hop and when they played their jingle, I remembered passing the place on Route 1 in Saugus, north of Boston last year when I went on a camping trip to Mount Chocorua in New Hampshire with the boy scouts. That seemed like a different life and thousands of miles away now.

By 11:00 pm the beer was gone, everyone was bored.

"William," Bobby announced. "Take me home."

I started the car but had to wait for Chico to get back in the rear and close the tailgate after taking a piss behind the hot dog shop. Everyone except me was feeling high. Chico was drunk. Two quarts of beer pushed him to the edge, and he was getting mouthy.

I headed back down Marine Road, planning on going to "M" Street park and leaving the car there. As I turned up "N" Street, not wanting to drive past the place I stole the car, there was a car approaching, headlights bright. Chico started yelling something and Bobby turned in the seat, pointed at Chico and screamed, "Shut the fuck up!" As Bobby turned, his left knee nudged my right leg and I twitched, pressing hard on the gas pedal. In and of itself, no problem, but I also involuntarily turned the steering wheel just enough to sideswipe the oncoming car. It wasn't much of a hit, but it was a hit.

Instinctively, I hit the brakes and looked back. That's when I saw the bubblegum machine on the roof. I had hit a cop car, a cruiser out of station #6.

"Go!" shouted Bobby. "Get out of here!" and I floored it going up two blocks and turning right. Halfway down the block I hit the brakes, threw it in PARK, yelled "Everyone out," and bailed out. Bobby had jumped before the car stopped rolling. Billy followed me out my door and Dizzy went out the passenger door. Chico had dropped the tailgate when we turned off "N" Street and jumped out long before the car stopped moving. Eddie crawled through the back and took off, ducking down behind the parked cars, heading back toward "N" Street.

Slipping between two cars, I tripped on the curb, going down hard on my right knee. The pain was excruciating. When I stood, I couldn't put weight on my leg, so started hopping down the street. That's when two cruisers appeared, one coming from each end of the block. Nowhere to go.

How ironic, the only sober one got caught. Both Bobby and Dizzy hid under parked cars until everything quieted down. The other three ran up an alley and jumped a few fences to get away.

The cells in station #6 were spartan, cells, not luxury rooms. I was scared, in a cell with two drunks, both passed out. Other than having me empty my pockets and taking my switchblade, nothing had happened. A big cop came in, a sergeant. He wiggled a finger at me and I followed him out to an empty cell at the end of the row.

"Sit down," he ordered, and I sat gingerly on the edge of the bunk, my knee swollen. "I talked to your father," which surprised me since I hadn't told him my name and I didn't carry any ID on me. Surprise must have registered on my face because he continued, "Yeah, we know who you are. Your brothers are a pain in the ass, like you, but your father is a good guy. He said he'd talk to the owner whose car you stole and work it out with him about paying for the damages."

I just sat and stared, afraid to say anything.

"Your father is worried that you're hanging around with the wrong crowd. Asked me if there's anything I could do to convince you to go in another direction."

"What did you tell him?"

"I told him, sure."

After a pause, I asked, "What did he say?"

"He said, 'I'll pick him up Sunday. Teach him to not take things that don't belong to him.'"

My head shriveled down into my shoulders and I started to pant, on the edge of panic.

Standing up, he walked out, saying, "stay put." Didn't even close the door. A minute later he came back carrying dingy gray coveralls. "Take off all your clothes and put this on," he ordered.

I stripped down and started to put on the coveralls when he interrupted. "Skivvies and socks too." When I complied, he rolled up my clothes in a bundle with the shoes in the middle and walked out.

I summoned the nerve to say, "I have to take a leak."

"Go ahead."

"There's no toilet."

He laughed, not a friendly sound, and said, "You're already learning."

I pissed in the corner of the cell away from the bunk, trying not to piss on my bare feet, then sat down on the edge of the bunk.

About half an hour went by. Other than the throbbing in my knee, I was beginning to relax, when the sergeant and another cop, bigger than the sergeant, came back, unlocked the door and saw the puddle of piss in the corner. The other cop stepped close to me, pointed at the puddle and said, "Clean it up."

Before I could reply, his right hand flicked out and a length of rubber hose, about two feet long, slashed me on my left arm. When I grabbed my left arm with my right, he hit that one. It hurt like hell, and I started to cry.

"No! No! Boy. Not yet. Plenty of time to cry later." And hit me again...and again...and again.

Every half hour or so, they came in and repeated the routine, sometimes they made me lean against the wall and they hit me on the back and across the back of my legs. It was rubber, and I wore the coveralls, so I never got cut, just bruised. I pissed myself more than once. Throughout the night, in between beatings, I could hear other activity, a few drunks yelling, but never saw anyone.

In the morning, a different cop came in, alone. He told me to take off my coveralls. Looking me over, he grunted, said, "Pull them back on," and left. In five minutes he returned with a tin cup of water, handed it to me through the bars and watched as I drank it. He reached for the empty cup and left, leaving me alone until the night shift came on.

Two cops again, different ones. They took turns whacking me with the rubber hose, every half hour, all night long, working on my legs and shoulders with an occasional punch to the gut. I puked twice but then there was nothing left to come up.

In the morning, the same day-shift cop came back. Same routine, drop your coveralls. This time, I heard him whisper "damn." He brought me another cup of water and a handful of saltine crackers. When he left, I tried to lie down on the bunk but any part of me that touched a hard surface hurt, so I ended up standing in the corner. My hands, they never hit my hands, head or feet, pressed against the wall to ease the pressure on my shoulder blades and ass.

Around noon, the sergeant showed up with the day-shift cop, the one who didn't hit me. He had me drop the coveralls, and I watched the sergeant shake his head. "Take him to the showers. Get him cleaned up and dressed," he said to the day-shift cop.

Taking a shower hurt. The water never got hot, room temperature at best, and rubbing soap on my shoulders and arms felt like sandpaper. Just flexing my arms hurt. Drying myself using a towel with the texture of a wood rasp, was agony.

Dressed, I waited in what was an interrogation room. I still stood, since my ass was so sore. At 2:00 pm, my father came in. I expected a tongue lashing and a long lecture; instead, he came over and gently hugged me. I stood there, bewildered, and cried.

As we went out, the sergeant who had observed a lot of the beatings but never participated, came over and said to my father, "There's no record of him ever being here. There's no report of a stolen car. There's only a vandalism of unknown origin report on the cruiser. I hope, for his sake and yours, we never see him here again."

My father's only comment, "I think he's learned his lesson."

He was right.

Ann Hymes

ONCE UPON A RIVER

I have come to expect the unexpected with my daughter Hannah. She marches through life with such optimism that events seem to adjust themselves to fit her pace. She is not daunted by the insurmountable. I have seen her parallel park a school bus towing a huge trailer stacked with eight-person river rafts. During college, Hannah worked as a white water rafting guide, squeezing rafting trips into week-ends and spending her summers on the river. Don't even think of telling her that girls can't do this sport.

Hannah has always been tall and fit, with strawberry hair flowing toward her waist. She smiles easily. In her rafting days, she looked relaxed in her wet suit and life jacket, but put her in a raft with swirling water and Class III or V rapids, and she was a master of concentration and strategy. Calling precise instructions to her paddlers, she navigated around boulders and through narrow and dangerous passages.

"This has to be a good run," Hannah explained with a laugh at the beginning of one trip. "My mother's on board!" It's an odd and wondrous feeling to have your child in charge. I listened carefully as she handed out helmets and explained the safety procedures and different paddling strokes.

Years of canoeing as a youngster with my brother flashed through my head. We never had a clue that strokes had names. We maneuvered around with the forward momentum of our own trial and error. Gentle lakes near Chicago had allowed great latitude for talent, but in Washington State, a good spring snow melt from the nearby mountains had created water deep and fast. This trip was not for the faint-hearted. There was a chorus of screaming as our raft lifted out of the river and crashed down with cold spray that drenched everyone.

Camaraderie develops quickly when strangers are thrown together with a common goal. We were the power for Hannah's directing. I watched her lean far back over the raft as she held the angle of her paddle against the current. Strength was necessary, but skill was in reading the water and making decisions that didn't wipe out the boat. Often she made broad, sweeping strokes to compensate for mistakes we novices had made.

"High side, left! High side!" she'd yell with urgency, and we all quickly slid over, changing the weight balance and allowing us to pass over an obstacle hidden in the water. Hannah's eyes scanned every direction, anticipating what was to come, while watchfully minding the safety of her passengers. "Hold on!" she'd call to someone who looked ready to pitch overboard. One less active paddler was preferable to retrieving a floating one.

Magnificent rock formations and towering pines reached high above us as we curved our way down stream. Hannah pointed out eagle nests and hidden caves and told stories of floods and Indian lore. She chatted and joked, learning about her fellow travelers and drawing us all together under the warm summer sun.

Being paid to do what you love is the ideal job in anyone's book. Hannah rowed crew in high school and was an expert sailor, but camp in Colorado had put the rushing descent of mountain rivers in her bones. For several years after college, when harsh northwestern winter months approached, Hannah looked around the world to see who was having summer. She didn't hesitate to get on a plane without the certainty of a job. Rafting in Nepal, Ecuador, and New Zealand filled the long gaps between seasons that left others snowbound. She defied the logic of regular employment for the wonder of unscripted adventure. Landing on the South Island of New Zealand, Hannah's new used van broke down, and an older couple stopped to help her. They took her home, and she lived with them for several days—even learning how to knit! The road to the river can be fraught with detours.

As Hannah developed expertise, becoming a senior guide and trip leader, I watched her nurture the desire to see others succeed. She organized rafting trips for inner city children and volunteered to take groups who were either blind or deaf, spacing them in ways they could help each other.

When my own rafting trip was over, and Hannah and the other guides were washing wet suits in big tubs, I walked over and put a $20 bill in her soapy hand. She got lots of tips that day. Once a group of professional football players had given her several hundred dollars; and once a shy, blind girl tucked a folded dollar bill under a stone and left it for her. They all got the best she had to offer.

The only time I've ever seen a triple rainbow, I was with this daughter of daring. Layers of beautiful arched beams filled the sky, reaching for the sun on a cloudy afternoon. I think rainbows follow Hannah, casting brilliant color and promise, and ending at her feet. We shared the awe of a triple rainbow that day, but when I'm with Hannah, I expect surprises.

Caroline Kalfas

SOGGY TOMATO SANDWICHES

While returning home from the local 4-H farm fair, my foot involuntarily eased off the gas as I glided past a local roadside stand with several cars parked in its half-moon, dirt driveway.

I glanced over to see what made the motorists stop and saw baskets of fresh South Jersey tomatoes lined up on the celery-green wooden shelves of the outdoor store front.

"I've got to get me some fresh, red tomatoes," I told myself and made a U-turn.

Garden tomatoes are about the best part of summer in South Jersey. I've seen area residents grow or buy tomatoes by the bushel to make their favorite sauce recipes and store the extraordinary flavors of the fruit in jars or in the freezer to use as a necessary culinary staple in their winter stews and pasta dishes.

Over the past few years, my teen-aged son and I have joined the frenzy, experimenting with tomatoes, peppers and onions from our garden. We've sliced, grated, chopped, and strained our way without recipes to create various tomato concoctions. Each bag of our frozen sauce tastes slightly different because of our let's-see-what's-in-the-cabinet, just-guess-how-much-to-use, and toss-it-in-why-not method of adding spices.

The haphazard, on-the-spot recipes eventually please our winter palates as we use the pre-cooked tomatoes as ingredients for various taco, stuffed pepper, chili, and meat sauces long after the local farm stands close their doors and cold weather sets in across the region.

But the best way to eat a fresh South Jersey tomato is to make a simple soggy tomato sandwich. I take two pieces of white bread (toasting is optional, depending on how soggy you like your sandwich); slather both slices with real mayonnaise (ideally, it's best to use Duke's Mayonnaise, but good luck finding Duke's in New Jersey); arrange sliced tomatoes on one of the mayonnaised bread squares and salt and pepper on the other. Put the slices together; lightly squish the sandwich with the palm of your hand; cut the sandwich into two or four pieces if you prefer; and enjoy a taste of the best sandwich ever. These homemade delicacies are good for breakfast, lunch, snack, supper, and midnight snack again. And if you grow your own tomatoes, you'll eat the sandwiches that often daily so the harvest won't go to waste.

Those who are new to the soggy tomato sandwich and wish to make one on their own should be advised to keep a napkin close by before taking the first bite of splendor because tomato juice mixed with mayonnaise from your sandwich is going to run down your fingers, into the palm and over the back of your hand. No matter if a person eats the sandwich whole or sliced in triangles, rectangles or squares, if the sandwich is made to perfection with the right amount of mayonnaise and fresh, juicy slices of tomato from the garden, the food is going to get slightly messy. But the eater won't care because the sandwich is that good. Second helpings are preferred.

Once in a while I splurge on bacon for a BT on toasted bread. Lettuce is another option with bacon for the common BLT. I've sprinkled my bread with cilantro or oregano, too. But honestly, nothing beats eating a soggy tomato sandwich with a napkin in your lap while seated underneath the shade of a screened-in porch, at a picnic table underneath the pines, or at the kitchen table in the heat of summer.

The tomatoes I planted this year remain green for now. But I've already shoved my toaster oven, electric mixer, and canisters of flour and sugar to the end of my kitchen counter to make room for all of the tomatoes I'll be harvesting once they ripen and turn red. The bread, mayonnaise, salt and pepper stand at the ready for the summertime all-you-can-eat soggy tomato sandwich marathon to begin.

And for any tomatoes that don't fit the plump and juicy standard of a well-made soggy tomato sandwich, they will become sauce.

POETRY

JAMIE BROWN

Stars

She called the constellations by the names
she gave them, knowing only that they ought
to have them. One of her invented games,
she called them gator, cypress, cloud, and caught
them in her fingers, stretched out overhead,
each word an image she had learned in school.
Naming them, thus, removed the nightly dread
of her life's thread unreeling from its spool.
While others played she met a man, and now
she names her children after days, and days
for years, her miseries for joys. The plow
in dreams leaves circles where these cattle graze;
death, childhood loss, abandonment, and the sound
of constellations as they circle round.

Small Consolation

(on viewing the painting "Compensation" by George Cochran Lambdin,
The Biggs Museum of American Art, Dover, Delaware)

The Union Army Officer, home
from the battlefront, disconsolate.
The young woman attends him.
A pillow, plate of cherries, fresh
flowers, and a book—is it poetry?
A bottle, nearly empty, neatly
stoppered, and the open window
with its distant, reddening sky.
Which vista holds him, the window-sash
framed view or her? She is troubled,
expectant. His raised legs rest upon
a shield-back chair, covered by
a crimson throw—perhaps it's only
one leg there. From what wound
is he recovering? Where are his troops?

How suppress the sounds of grape
and the chains fired from Parrott guns
as they rip through the flesh and bone of
his comrades, their bodies bursting
like over-ripe melons? Their cries
for "Mother" and the comfort of childhood
as they die echo insistently inside his
hollow skull. The sounds of the screams in
hospital tents as doctors' saws remove
limbs shattered by miniballs—hell, the sounds

of the saws alone could drive one mad.

Are his arms stacked for good against
this new infirmity? The tropical birds
in the cage above suggest so. Lovebirds?
They do not look it. The woman
wonders where he wanders in his mind.
Isn't she enough for him? All this and her.

She can never know. She is no consolation.

TARA A. ELLIOTT

Imprint

I wonder if they come with the soul,
these circular impressions
—spirals so distinct
no one shares the same swirls,
the same ridges of skin.

These are mine—
they tell the trail of me
in the soft pads of fingertips,
the wisps of lines left on objects,
left on lives.

WENDY ELIZABETH INGERSOLL

My Life as a Pianist

My cousin calls to propose
a medley of our farms, purpose

to create habitat for quail.
Everyone should just play Bach,
I advise. Polyphony is the answer:

acres intermix, lush layers and thus
cover composed. I collapse in the hammock,

consider what is God's plan for quail.
My dog sprawls on the crabgrass and pants.

She's thirsty for Bach: cantatas, partitas,
she's not particular. I time my inhale

to her metered exhale. My dog pretends
she doesn't see the deer nibbling at our corn,
like me pretending to fish off the point,

really just watching bait.
She cartwheels her legs: is she recalling

the day my large hands picked her from the litter?
She never saw her mom again. I lean

back into the hammock as land locks down for dusk,
hear a sighing in the corn,
            then: *bobwhite, bobwhite*—

does God plan out these themes and variations,
or is everything improv?

Necessary Predators

Lay your head where liars sleep,
listen for their mutter,
is it something you've heard before? Swim
for undertone,

skip backwash where needle skirrs from record
and all we catch is empty disc-spin, soto voce,
wind and waves breaking on barren reef:

Christmas Island— natives overfished the sharks, snappers,
leaving empty
atolls: ecological malfunction,

smaller fish treading fearful in their eerie altered scape.
      What we want is

murderers, menacers, lying knaves and thieves,
to balance out our roiling shoal – what is Bethlehem after all

without Herod, Easter without Judas.

Photo of My Father and the Wild Goose

He pins its wings wide on an upslope, shotgun
tilted against the springhouse
camouflaged by shadow: my father

was a killer of wild birds, a builder of sanctuary ponds:
he gazes father-like at the sprawled goose,
feathers unfurling, left breast exposed,

down and quill curved like a fountain, my father's fist
coiled above as if
plucking pellets from a heart. I remember

him reaching to embrace me, me tilting backward,

not knowing that if flight was ever called for in my life
I'd best have flown not away,
but toward.

CYNTHIA A. INGRAM

Down "Y" Ocean

My sisters call and ask, "How about a few days together in O.C."

One step out of the car sails me head-on into the wind;
ocean breezes
threaten to push me away from the condo
instead playfully draw me inside.

My first walk is close to the churning water.
The shoreline and my stroll span out toward the meeting of sky and land.
My underused leg muscles grouch against the uneven fine pebbles.
Several loud bright shells catch my eye and I move beyond my thoughts.

The waves roll in relentless crashing cymbals;
their weight, a clap of thunder, smacks the hard surface.
The roar, the ripples, and the rhythm are background music for my rumination,
I rush back to memories of other times.

My knowing moves out past my experiences;
I am thrown forward, tossed backward.
I drown in my tragedies;
rise up in my triumphs.
My day to day rhythms lift me;
I move shell by shell
down my own beach to breathtaking horizons.

Winter Warmth

Fall leaves lovely colors in puddles all around.
Winter, cold, crisp and bitter, is bearing down.

Before the winds sneak down the chimney,
and the mice move in 'til May;
gather warmth instead of firewood,
warmth of friends and family love;
light of laughter and of memories.
Snuggle down;
pull them in,
all the ones who need joy,
smiles and hugs,
and a mug of sweetness by the fire.

MARGARET FARRELL KIRBY

How to Plant a Flowering Garden

Imagine your garden. Sketch its shape.
A blank canvas waiting for you. Fill it
with a rainbow of colors, outrageous blossoms
mingled with delicate. Annuals and perennials to last
the season. Plant flowers that attract

butterflies, bees, and hummingbirds.
Purple coneflowers. Yellow and orange daylilies.
Deep red zinnias. Petunias and pansies
in hues of blue, pink,
and lavender. Plant with

abandon. Pretend—you are still
an unruly teenager, heedless
of perfection,
not caring
        if you stay in the border.

Let your flowers teach you
about pruning and the art
of letting go.
Learn their moods and their needs. Help them
to flourish. Remember to visit in light and

in shadow, on your good days and
when you are hanging
by a thread

Your garden will welcome you. Loyally.
Silently. Something may

awaken.
Something precious you thought you had
lost
but was hushed, dormant,
waiting.

When your last petal droops and your branches
wither, as summer fades and fragrance
flees, when tender leaves turn brown and brittle,
and the earth is silenced by winter's
barrenness,

imagine your garden biding its time. Waiting
for darkness to lift. For spring's sun
to hover. For a time to plant.
Imagine. A dormant canvas waiting
for your return.

BARBARA LOCKHART

First Lesson on Time

All summer we watched
(while we were doing other things)
the field of soybeans flourish, round
green leaves fluttering to fullness,
and then, for three brief days in September,
turn gold while the grackles flew in
as in Van Gogh's last painting, their
hovering blackness an
interruption above the golden field.
Then the leaves fell and the lonely pod-bearing
stalks stood rust-colored and dry
until the combines came
like armored tanks before the promised rain,
making us run for the porch cushions while an
orange cloud rose and the fragile stalks
gave way to machines with snouts
like elephant trunks to pour the golden
beans into the beds of silver trucks.
My grandson pressed his face against the glass
of the kitchen door and safely watched the giant's teeth
just yards from the house now—comb through the
stalks and suck them up
as it huffed and puffed, sending
billows of bean dust into the air,
stirring his three-year-old's wonder
at summer's decisive end
and the clean sweep of the harvested field
like his chalkboard, erased, and waiting
for another season.

Peaches

The sun enflames bared arms and faces
as we swing the wooden ladder
through the weeds.
Peaches, overripe and tender, tremble
when I pull the branches earthward
and reach beyond arm's length
while you, my daughter, steady
the ladder. Some fall to the old shed
roof and roll, muffled, down the tin
like childhood's padded feet.
You laugh at the sound, arms
outstretched, receiving peaches.

We each have work: me, culling
along the branches, shadowed hands
curled and veined, encasing every peach
like gifts to you, who
with eager waiting fingers,
complete the arc to earth as golden
hairs glimmer on sunburned skin.

The unbroken circle—
from root to bark,
the blossom bearing,
the careful passing
down of ripened fruit
is brief
as the slipping sun at dusk
and done too soon.

Alora, Ocean City

Before this day becomes yesterday
I want to write you down—
pouring a cup of ocean
from your paper teapot
and tasting the sand,
now chocolate marshmallow
as you said, *We're*
just pretending,
to a passerby.

Before this day becomes yesterday
I want to hold it, grain by grain
and pour by pour,
the sugar and the lemon of it,
the cakes topped with bottle caps,
your brown and eager body,
your hair tossing
side to side as
down to the ocean
you ran to fill a cup
of tea for me.

I will always remember
and when I fade
I'd like you to remember
but I know you are too young.
Yet I like to think that
down in the silent,
loving part of you,
you might always harbor

the love that poured from me to you
that morning
as I brushed your hair
and tied it with a purple ribbon.

Tell me a story, you said,
and had me wrap you in the pink
towel because it was
your favorite color—
and then you sat
in my lap, waiting.

I began: *Once there was a*
little sea gull—
No! you said.
Tell me a story about
Omie and Alora.
And so I said,
One day, Omie and Alora
went to the boardwalk
and Omie pushed Alora
in the blue stroller with the
hood to keep the sun off
and Omie said,
"Wouldn't it be fun
to dress up and have our picture taken?"
And Alora said, "Where?"
And Omie said, "Here! At the
Old Timey Photo shop.
See all the pretty dresses?"

So, for real, we dressed up
in laces and ruffles and hats
(pink, of course)
and smiled together

looking into the camera,
pretending yesterday,
and marking today
for all the tomorrows.

Now tell about that sound!
you said, as the foghorn
sent its patient signal
and I said,
It's only to keep the ships safe
from the rocks,
knowing full well
it was really Time
with its witless clamor
and patient persistence
that would wear away the day
like the drawings we made on the sand
of you and a cat with feather whiskers
and a pony that looked like a dog—
which you never minded—smiled at
anyway—and had me draw
you in the sandy saddle.

CLAIRE MCCABE

Lyndon Johnson and Beagle "Him"

Loyal as a dog

To his departed master

(that much-loved president

cut down in his prime),

heavy with grief

in his accidental office,

burdened by unsought duties,

Johnson stumbled.

He tugged on "Him's" ears

to hear the beagle bay

and give melodious tongue.

The public protested; they couldn't see

his eyes, deep and lost,

face drawn into folds.

He needed the howl of a hound

to call him home:

days of rabbits and rifles,

hounds and hikes,

fields far from pavement,

from motorcades.

And after the hunt,

a warm spot by the fire,

to circle and settle and pine

for innocent gunshot.

NANCY MCCLOY

Counting Backwards

Paper is appropriate for beginnings—

Hallmark suggests it as a one year

anniversary gift. He gave her a red paper

valentine—handmade. A poem he wrote

was included. It read: *this heart is flat*

but my love is not. She wasn't sure

what he meant, then or now.

Cotton is listed as a second year gift.

Useful for all the tears she cried about that time.

Crystal and glass were perfect choices

for year three. Their marriage was starting

to crack. Nothing they tried seemed

to glue it back together.

Flowers were his gift year four. It was clear

by then that he wanted no fruits from their marriage.

She should have known.

Paper, first and last gift of their married life.

Valentines and divorce decrees weigh about the same.

JANE MILLER

Stranger

after Jo McDougall

When happiness came to visit,

I invited him in. He drank

the best wine, all the beer

in the garage refrigerator.

I would have thought

he would not need such an escape.

But turns out, he has a hard job.

He has to steer conversations clear

of all grief. He has to be jolly.

He thought I would be happy

to feed him steak and pommes frites

in the French manner— a salade verte

and Costco cream puffs for good measure.

They are good, but I had

to set limits. Ours is a double bed

and I am a married woman with a dog.

Caesarian

I held her captive, suspended in a diving bell

as if to shelter from calamity this child

inside me like an organ I couldn't live without,

for every birth begins a eulogy.

But they cut her loose from the bubble

where I had talked to her,

where she tapped

morse code for months.

Post-delivery, they sewed her absence into a finish line.

Every year after: a racing bib

with candles for numbers.

I let her go as I should,

but let no one tell you it is easy.

The wound where once I cradled her

a buckled scar.

MARY EMMA TISINGER

By the Hearth

His chair, with stripes of burgundy, green
and tan, (not so straight now, after years
of being leaned against,
or sat upon),
still hugs the space nearby.
The smothering odor of wood smoke
lingers,
while the glass enclosure, shut when he left
and never reopened,
reflects the light of the reading lamp
on the table by the side.
My eyes begin to sting
and blur,
as yet, I see him
sitting there.

Come Christmas, I'll put pine cones and holly
on the mantle.

Barrett Warner Comes to Dover

I drove to *Roma's*,
wondering . . .
would I be glad in the doing?
I was not disappointed.
He looked like someone
who *could* plant horses
and watch them grow,
which he said he does, but
he spoke as poets speak.
Scattered Van Gogh's and Picasso's
around the room with his words,
and seemed like an old friend
in less than an hour. Not in the least
someone you would turn off
and draw daisies and tulips
on your napkin.
And he did all this
with a hand once kicked off
by a horse.

August Storm

Sounded like a blast,
that rumble . . .
heavy, deep,
just before the rain.
Could have been a car
banging into another
(happens sometimes),
or maybe an explosion
nearby.
But then the rain came down.

Poured from the roof,
so much so
the gutters overflowed,
and the maples and yews out front,
trembled;
while the leaves flew all around,
searching frantically
for a place to settle
on the wet, soggy
ground.

PAT VALDATA

What We're Dealt

Face it: you can't read the future
in postcards. No matter how many times
you shuffle and deal, no gypsy turns
one over and says, "You'll never
get a tongue stud." It's as dull
as an old saw, this old saw, and
universal: Your yesterdays predict
your tomorrows. You have more
foreknowledge than the fake psychic
in Fells Point who, come to think
of it, did foretell you'd meet the tall
blond man whose name begins with R.

Dream Geography

It's an elastic world
where the laws of physics
only more or less apply.
One minute you're walking
in a backyard. The next,
you're on some beach. You
become all sorts of characters:
a teacher, lost and late for class;
a consultant walking through
a revolving door, naked;
your mother, unaware she died
twenty years before. Your childhood parakeet Skippy chirps
on your left shoulder
just before tornados roll
in a pack across flat terrain
you have never seen.
You're driving city streets
in a Salisbury that can't
exist except in your
dream-addled brain, always
shifting into the right lane
of the same expressway,
taking the same exit, the one
leading to a bridge with no end.

All Good Things

How soon our affair has ended!
Did we love each other at all
From late spring to early fall?
Fingertips extended,
Our hands blended,
We leaned against the sea wall.
Who said it first, do you recall?
Perhaps if we had we attended
More to hope, we might have done
The love thing better. Let's not forget,
I said, you were the one
Who loved me first, yet
You looked out toward the sun,
Your face hard, your mind set.

LYNNE SPIGELMIRE VITI

Girls, 1959

We never sensed privilege in the air we breathed.

We thought— were taught—if life wasn't fair, at least

our parents, teachers were. The President was.

We believed all men were equal, women too—

we could be lawyers, pilots, doctors, reporters

if we just put our minds to it.

We thought the woman who came five days of seven

to do our wash, clean bathrooms, cook our meals

was like family— we never asked why

she never married, lived downtown

in a cramped apartment we visited only once.

I saw a wide Windsor rocking chair that used to be ours,

a blond wood bed from Sears our family gave her.

I peered out her living room window to

the movie theater across the street, its name—

The Roosevelt—in orange neon lights. A colored theater,

we called it. The front wall of yellow bricks,

flakes of peeling paint dotting the sidewalk.

She took the city bus. We rode in our car or a taxi.

Summer nights, heat stalled over the harbor, suffused the city—

our Chevrolet glided across town through neighborhoods

of people sitting on front stoops fanning themselves,

drinking iced tea from glasses robed in condensation.

Grownups watched over shirtless boys screaming,

dancing in white water spewed from hydrants,

cold city water shooting onto black asphalt.

The Summer People in Winter

Near Uncle Tim's bridge stands

a dwarf tree with twisted branches, tiny

white blossoms about to fall—

white sand, shells of horseshoe crabs, not as many

as in years past. Matted salt hay, soft underfoot.

Across the marsh, the old cannery-turned-

yoga studio by the fish shack, empty parking lot,

freshly paved with crushed oyster shells,

bleached, pristine, waiting for the summer people.

In winter they stay in their houses, reading the paper.

Some sit at the piano, plunk out a few tunes.

They write letters to the editor, eschewing

email, preferring paper, envelope, self-adhesive stamps.

They walk their letters to the mailbox,

wait for the metal clank as the missives disappear

into the blue container— pickup, 4 PM.

The summer people in winter wear

their good coats to the opera, don

sports gear for the hockey games.

They go to work early, they're the last to leave the office.

They stand for O Say Can You See and O Canada.

They lug their groceries in reusable bags. They

watch the calendar, dreaming of the marsh,

the kettle ponds' clear water, the warm waves

late August afternoons on the bay beach,

shell-cluttered sand near the rock jetty, a fat orange sun

slow dancing down to the horizon.

Elegy for Alice

Your brain bled out on one side, then the other.

It sent faint messages to your lungs—

orders that grew fainter, like a fading telegraph

in a sinking vessel on a distant sea,

emitting weak dots and dashes till all went silent.

Your brothers, their wives, your sister and your mother,

your children sat in Adirondack chairs

on the green lawn of your new house

the one you worked so hard to paint,

to get the feng shui perfect—

Tree branches formed a heart against the sky.

Your work was watching the stage, describing

every detail the sighted noticed.

We asked who'd now explain to the blind

what the actors were doing when

they entered a living room or stood atop a fake mountain

to sing a paean to the American experiment, or to a beloved.

Last summer you admired my magenta shirt

the one that caused the hummingbirds to divebomb me

when I wore it into the garden on August mornings.

I wish I'd given it to you on the spot, so you could've

drawn hummingbirds too, watch their beating wings,

in the fleeting, full-flowered summer garden.

CONTRIBUTORS

Maisha D. Britt currently resides in Clayton, NC. She joined SWORD and ESWA while living in Dover, Delaware. She is a Clinical Christian Therapist and an Elections Precinct Official in Wake County, North Carolina. Her poems have been featured in anthologies including The National Library of Poetry, Famous Poets Society, Famous Poets of the 20th Century, and Noble House. She has been selected to receive the 2018 Albert Nelson Marquis Lifetime Achievement Award.

Jamie Brown is author of *Sakura, Conventional Heresies,* and *Freeholder and Other Poems*. He founded *The Broadkill Review* and is CEO of The Broadkill River Press, based in Milton, Delaware. His poetry, fiction and non-fiction have been widely published and he taught at Wesley College and University of Delaware after twelve years teaching at GWU. He taught the first Poetry workshop at the Smithsonian, and helped edit several magazines. He was Poetry Critic for *The Washington Times.*

Charles Brent Cole is a retiree who lives in Salisbury, Maryland. "Boundaries" is his first published work. He is currently working on a memoir and says he is testing out Plato's saying, "The unexamined life is not worth living." He got the idea from writing "Boundaries," which he wrote to make peace with the incident it describes. It's his hobby, he says, so you may or may not ever hear from him again.

Jackson Coppley is an award-winning writer. His career spans senior positions in the Bell System and IBM to the launch of his own software company. Now a full-time writer, his work focuses on relationships and adventure. Coppley and his wife Ellen, divide their time between homes in Rehoboth Beach, Delaware, and Chevy Chase, Maryland. Other works by Coppley include *Leaving Lisa,* a novel; and *Tales from our Near Future,* a collection of short stories.

Walter F. Curran is a retired Merchant Mariner and the current Mayor of Ocean View, DE. He has sailed and worked on the docks in Boston, Philadelphia, Baltimore, Jacksonville and San Juan, P.R. A member of the Eastern Shore Writers Association. Rehoboth Beach Writer's Guild, and Maryland Writer's Association, Walt has self-published two novels, *Young Mariner* and *On to Africa*, and a book of poetry, *Slices of Life-Cerebral spams of the soul.* His website is www.walterfcurran.com.

Tara A. Elliott lives with her husband and son in Salisbury, Maryland where she teaches English. She is the founder and director of Salisbury Poetry Week, is honored to serve as Maryland Humanities Teacher of the Year, and is a facilitator for Salisbury University's Lighthouse Literary Guild. Her recent poems have been published in *MER*, *The TAOS Journal of International Poetry & Art*, and *Wildness*, *Triggerfish* and *The American Journal of Poetry,* among others.

David Healey lives in Chesapeake City, Maryland and spent 21 years as a newspaper reporter and editor, mostly in Cecil County. He is the author of three nonfiction books on regional history, including *Delmarva Legends & Lore*, as well as several novels. He serves on the board of the Eastern Shore Writers' Association and is a contributing editor for the International Thriller Writers magazine. Visit him online at www.davidhealeyauthor.com.

David J. Hoffman is a Scientist Emeritus ecotoxicologist with the U.S. Geological Survey. He lives in Bivalve, Maryland and also spends time in Old Lyme, CT as a trustee for the Florence Griswold Museum. He is the author of over 175 scientific publications including books, book chapters, and reviews. He has served on multiple editorial boards. *Handbook of Ecotoxicology* was a best seller for CRC Press. He has written a series of humorous short stories.

Frank E Hopkins writes realistic crime novels and short stories portraying social and political issues. He has published three novels: *Unplanned Choices, The Opportunity,* and *Abandoned Homes: Vietnam Revenge Murders,* which won first place in the mystery/thriller category in the Maryland Writers Association 2018 novel contest. Frank's collection of short stories, *First Time,* was awarded second place for a collection by a single author in the Delaware Press Associations 2017 Communication contest.

Ann Hymes was born and raised in the Midwest. She graduated from Mills College in Oakland, California, with a B.A. in English. While living in St. Michaels, Maryland, she went back to graduate school and received an M.A. in English from Washington College. She has published creative nonfiction on the *Christian Science Monitor* Home Forum page, and her novel *Shadow of Whimsy: A Cape Cod Love Story* was published by Secant Publishing. It is also available from Amazon, Apple, and Audible as an audiobook. Ann can be reached at whimsytowers@gmail.com.

Wendy Elizabeth Ingersoll is a retired piano teacher, AKA Wendy Perry. She lives in Newark, Delaware, and also spends time at a family property near Chestertown, Maryland. Publications include her book *Grace Only Follows* (National Federation of Press Women Prize); two chapbooks; poems in *Poetry East*, *Naugatuck River Review*, *Connecticut River Review*, *Cahoodaloodaling*, *Mojave River Review*, *The Lyric*, and others. She was a Finalist for the 2015 Dogfish Head Poetry Prize. She serve as a reader for *The Delmarva Review*. See wendyingersoll.com.

Cynthia A. Ingram, a retired researcher, lives in Denton, Maryland. She is a life-long writer, although only published in employee newsletters and in a *Star-Democrat* Valentine poem. She loves her family, friends, the Eastern Shore, and books. She is a member of the Write-On group of writers that meet to share their writing on a chosen topic. They meet at the Foundry in Denton at 6:00 p.m. on the second and fourth Tuesdays of each month. She can be reached at ingram47c@gmail.com.

Caroline Kalfas is a freelance writer and former newspaper journalist who lives in Woolwich Township, New Jersey. She helped establish the *Watering Can*, a seasonal newsletter for the Woolwich Community Garden. A graduate of N.C. State University in Raleigh, she is a member of several writers' groups and organizations, including the Eastern Shore Writers Association. Read more of her essays about gardening at greenthumbchatter.wordpress.com.

Margaret Farrell Kirby is a member of the Rehoboth Beach Writer's Guild and the Eastern Shore Writers Association. A memoir piece and two short stories of hers have been published in *Beach Life, The Boardwalk, and The Beach House.* Her poetry appeared in *The Divine Feminine, An Anthology of Seaside Scribes*. She divides her time between Silver Spring, Maryland and Rehoboth Beach, Delaware.

Brent Lewis is a native Eastern Shoreman with local roots going back generations. He has written for magazines, newspapers, and newsletters, and for a decade oversaw the Kent Island Heritage Society's Oral History Program. He's published two nonfiction books, *Remembering Kent Island: Stories from the Chesapeake* and *A History of the Kent Island Volunteer Fire Department*, and one novel, *Bloody Point 1976*. Brent blogs regularly at easternshorebrent.com, and can be contacted at whiterubberboot@gmail.com.

Living on a farm in Rhodesdale, Maryland, **Barbara Lockhart** uses the setting of the Eastern Shore for her novels, *Requiem for a Summer Cottage* and *Elizabeth's Field* (Independent Book Publishers silver medal winner 2014), as well as for her collection of short stories, *The Night is Young (*Indie Excellence Book Awards finalist, 2017). Her children's books celebrate Shore life in such titles as *Rambling Raft, Once a Pony Time, Mosey's Field*, and *Will's Tractor*. Her first publication,

Read to me, Talk with me, written during her teaching career, is a manual used nationwide to encourage parents to read to their children. For more information see www.barbaramarielockhart.com.

Lynne Lockhart is a painter whose work explores the Eastern Shore landscape, farms, people and wildlife. Her paintings are included in public, private, and museum collections throughout the United States. The cover image of *Bay to Ocean 2018*, "Derelicts," is an oil painting inspired by a scene in the outer marshes of Chincoteague Island, Virginia. To see more work or to contact the artist go to lynnelockhart.com.

Claire McCabe splits her time between homes in Delaware and Maryland, living with three cats, two dogs, and a life partner. She teaches writing at the University of Delaware and writes poetry with both on-line and local writing groups—loving every minute of it. She will receive her MFA in poetry in January, 2019, from the Solstice program at Pine Manor College.

Nancy McCloy has been interested in writing since her childhood in southwestern Pennsylvania. She moved to the Eastern Shore of Maryland after college and enjoyed a career as an educator. After retiring, she joined a writer's group and was included in two self-published collections. She is a member of a small poetry salon and recently had three poems, one an honorable mention, accepted into a show at River Arts in Chestertown. She and her husband live in Still Pond.

Jane Miller's poetry has appeared in the *Iron Horse Literary Review, Summerset Review, cahoodaloodaling, Mojave River Review* and *Pittsburgh Poetry Review*, among others. A nominee for Best New Poets and Best of the Net, she received a 2014 grant from the Delaware Division of the Arts. She was a finalist in the 2016 IHLR chapbook contest and the 2017 Red Wheelbarrow Poetry Contest. She lives in Wilmington.

W. Scott Olsen is a professor of English at Concordia College in Moorhead, Minnesota, where he also edits the literary journal *Ascent*. He is the author of eleven books and co-editor of three anthologies, most recently *A Moment with Strangers* (NDSU Press 2016). His individual essays have appeared in journals such as *Kenyon Review*, *North American Review*, *Alaska Quarterly Review*, *North Dakota Quarterly*, and *Huffington Post*. Also a photographer, his work appears frequently in Lensculture.com and Terrain.org.

Russell Reece's poems, stories and essays have appeared in a variety of journals and anthologies. He has received fellowships in literature from The Delaware Division of the Arts and the Virginia Center for the Creative Arts. His stories and poetry have received Best of the Net nominations, awards from the Delaware Press Association, the Faulkner-Wisdom competition and others. Russ lives in rural Sussex County near Bethel, Delaware on the beautiful Broad Creek. You can learn more at his website, russellreece.com.

Southern-born, from the foothills of the North Carolina mountains, **Mary Emma Tisinger** now calls the flatlands of Delaware home. Her poetry and other writings have appeared in various magazines, publications, and books; her latest, an inspirational book, *Through the Leaves that Fall*, is available through Amazon. She looks forward to the release of her children's book, *Bumpity, Bumpity, Bump—No Nap for Anthony*, by late summer or early fall.

Pat Valdata is a poet and novelist with an MFA in writing from Goddard College. Her publications include two poetry books, *Where No Man Can Touch* (winner of the 2015 Donald Justice Poetry Prize) and *Inherent Vice*; the chapbook *Looking for Bivalve*; and two novels, *Crosswind* and *The Other Sister*. She is an adjunct professor who teaches creative writing for the University of Maryland University College and the Salisbury University Lighthouse Literary Guild. She lives in Crisfield, Maryland.

Lynne Spigelmire Viti, born and raised in Baltimore, spent many a summer in Ocean City, Maryland, crabbing, fishing and jumping the waves. A senior lecturer emerita at Wellesley College, she is the author of *Baltimore Girls (*2017) and *The Glamorganshire Bible (2018*), both from Finishing Line Press, and a microchapbook, *Punting* (Origami Poems Project, 2018). She was awarded Honorable Mentions in the Joe Gouveia Outermost Poetry Contest (2018), Concrete Wolf Louis Chapbook competition (2017), and Allen Ginsberg Poetry Competition (2015).

She blogs at stillinschool.wordpress.com.

Made in the USA
Columbia, SC
12 September 2018